April 2021
To My dear
Aunt Mary
"Dogwood Johnny's"
Sister,

That Southern Thing

I hope you
& your family enjoy
my little story about
my wonderful dad
- it begins on page 5.
I love & admire you. As
with my dad, your faith
inspires me. love,
Mary Anne

Personal Story Publishing Project Series

Bearing Up, 2018
Exploring, 2019

Other titles by Randell Jones

Scoundrels, Rogues, and Heroes of the Old North State, 2004 & 2007
   by Dr. H.G. Jones, edited by Randell Jones & Caitlin Jones

In the Footsteps of Daniel Boone, 2005
   with *On the Trail of Daniel Boone* (companion DVD), 2005

In the Footsteps of Davy Crockett, 2006 (out of print)

Before They Were Heroes at King's Mountain, 2011

A Guide to the Overmountain Victory National Historic Trail, 2011,
   second edition, 2016

Trailing Daniel Boone, DAR marking Daniel Boone's Trail, 1912-1915,
   2012

The Daniel Boone Wagon Train—a journey through The Sixties, 2013

Interactive, Online Tour of the Overmountain Victory NH Trail, 2014
   (link from www.danielboonefootsteps.com)

Interactive, Online Tour of Daniel Boone's Trail, 2015
   (link from www.danielboonefootsteps.com)

The American Spirit, 1780, 2016 (free YouTube video)
   (link from www.danielboonefootsteps.com)

From Time to Time in North Carolina, 2017

Available through Daniel Boone Footsteps
www.danielboonefootsteps.com
1959 N. Peace Haven Rd., #105
Winston-Salem, NC 27106

That Southern Thing

Randell Jones. editor

Daniel Boone Footsteps
Winston-Salem, North Carolina

Everyone in the South has no time for reading
because they are all too busy writing.
— William Faulkner

Preface

This book is the third in a series of annual collections of personal stories on a set theme, our Personal Story Publishing Project. We began in 2018 with ***Bearing Up***, a collection of 45 stories on the theme of "making do, bearing up, and overcoming adversity." For our second collection in 2019, ***Exploring***, our writers shared stories of "exploring—discoveries, challenges, and adventure," again true stories from their own lives and sometimes from the lives of ancestors or family members.

The book you are holding is the result of our third Call for Personal Stories, this on the theme: "That Southern Thing—living, loving, laughing, loathing, leaving the South." We thank the dozens and dozens of writers who responded to the call by submitting such interesting, thoughtful, and well-crafted stories. They delivered the diversity and depth of perspective we were hoping for and the humor and insight which proved we chose the right theme. Each story is limited to 800 words, so the writers where challenged in executing their craft, telling an interesting story succinctly.

We received submissions from writers in North Carolina, South Carolina, Kentucky, Arkansas, Tennessee, Alabama, Washington, Florida, Illinois, and New York. We wish we could have printed them all, but we are delighted to continue sharing at least 45 in this collection.

In 2019, we launched a second outlet for sharing the work of these fine writers with a broader audience. Their work can now be heard in our weekly podcast, "6-minute Stories." It is available through Apple Podcasts (iTunes), Spotify, and Stitcher. You can listen directly to "6-minute Stories" and find all the stories archived at **RandellJones.com**.

That Southern Thing, the Personal Story Publishing Project, and "6-minute Stories" podcast are undertaken by author and publisher Randell Jones, doing business as Daniel Boone Footsteps in Winston-Salem, North Carolina.

Thank you for enjoying and appreciating good storytelling. And, remember . . .
Everybody loves a good story.[sm] •

RJ

Contents

Contents

xi

Contents

Introduction

"That Southern thing" is a curious notion. It has no meaning other than what one ascribes to it from one's experiences, what one's heard, what one's read, what one has come, in turn, to believe to be the case. And for that reason, we thought this theme was perfect for our Personal Story Publishing Project and ripe for exploring: "That Southern thing—living, loving, laughing, loathing, leaving the South."

I remember hearing that during the presidential campaign of Jimmy Carter, some of the secret service detail showed up in Plains, Georgia, in the heart of peanut country, dressed in overalls with straw hats and blades of long grass dangling in their teeth, thinking that was how to blend in unnoticed in the Deep South. I don't know if that was a true story or just one that circulated for the amusement of us Southerners. But we knew most certainly that "those not from around here" labored under serious prejudices toward and misconceptions of "the South."

I was born in the South and have never lived farther north than Winston-Salem, where I live now. It's been Little Rock,

Memphis, Atlanta, Chapel Hill, and now home. It's been west to east, backtracking my Welsh ancestors' apparent responses since 1668 Virginia to the luring promise of opportunity always just a little farther west. Neither my ancestors nor I have done much south to north.

The real changes, of course, have come with time and technology and temperament, not latitude. I was born when Harry Truman was president, came of age with the assassination of John F. Kennedy, watched on a portable TV from my Georgia Tech dormitory Neil Armstrong step onto the moon. A decade-and-a-half later, I moved to Winston-Salem where the sweet aroma of tobacco being processed wafted over downtown, smelling like money, as it had for a hundred years. The first local restaurant to offer a non-smoking section felt to some like a cultural affront. But it wasn't, of course. Times change and they will continue to do so, but at their own pace. Just last year our community changed the name of its Dixie Classic Fair. Some were appalled, some applauded. And, so it goes. The South is sweet and slow but also rowdy and contentious. It's contradictory, selective in its certainty but also open to what might be coming next. The South is a curiosity.

That Southern Thing

We were gratified by the response to our Call for Personal Stories, and we are grateful to all who invested time and energy into crafting personal stories for possible inclusion in this anthology. From among the submissions, we chose stories to include based on the quality of the writing and the resonance of the personal experiences shared with the theme.

The stories presented here are a testament that good story-telling is alive and well. Some will make you wince, some laugh out loud, and some cause you to drift into your own recollections to ponder the experience. We do indeed hope that your own personal stories will come to mind. We hope also that you might write them down, share them in your own circles of friends and family, and invite those folks to do the same.

We are sharing in this collection stories of reflection and remembrance, stories of contrast and comparison, stories of then and now, of what is, what was, and what some hope might be or fear is on its way. In the pages which follow, we are treated to stories of praise for an inspirational parent, of a grandparent's life-changing love, of the proclivities of a favorite aunt, and of warnings about those we would rather forget. We encounter stories of living with full-blown discrimination, hate out in public, and prejudice disguised as a social norm. We meet delightful characters in vignettes described from childhood, find true love that endures, and enjoy memories of childhood adventures and courage unfettered. We find people bringing life into this world, making their own way in this world, and saying goodbye to this world too soon.

Some stories are about the perils of Southern parenting, the hazards of Southern culture. Others are about dealing with greed and grumpiness, struggling to see ourselves as others see us, exploring the Southern mystique, the particular, the problematic. Some are remembering splendid plates and recipes and those who made those dishes unforgettable. Others have us finding our way in a strange land and discovering we have arrived home. We are revisiting and correcting the stories of a history we thought we knew, discovering what we cannot see ourselves, and hoping for change, assuring ourselves without proof that it will be better. We are embracing the unique, confronting the ugly, remembering the stories that make our families special. We are recalling characters who taught us more than we knew at the time, staying brave and strong, and knowing that love wins out eventually.

From this collection of stories, the writers begin to know themselves as Southerners—newly arrived or never left; they reveal to the reader some indication of what that was, what it is, and what it yet might be. In that manner, these writers humbly, respectfully assure those curious souls not from around here, "Don't worry. It's that Southern thing." •

RJ

One Southerner's Legacy
by Janice Luckey

A "knot on a log," a "tough old bird"—some descriptions of my grandfather, the undisputed patriarch of our family. Indeed, he was a scrawny Hercules, a farmer and a mill hand, who brought his wife, daughter, and extended family out of the Georgia cotton fields for the promise of better jobs in North Carolina.

He was an arrangement of bones fashioned into a stick of a man with gnarled leather skin, wrinkled and worn like a pair of old work gloves. Most of his face was taken up by a large nose, hooked and humped by too many breaks. Weathered and stooped like a good work horse, he blended naturally into the sepia landscape of fertile soil and dried corn husks.

Grandpa never just walked. His gait was like a colt trotting, skittish to be on to the next task, denim overalls flapping around skinny legs. After working the farm since 5 a.m., he came in for a bite of lunch—Crowder peas, whatever meat was left from breakfast and a biscuit. He drew sustenance mainly from "Co' Cola," aspirin, and Maalox, a Winston always burning between crooked fingers.

After lunch a nap, then on to sweat out the second shift at the mill as he did for 30 years, retiring with a paltry $25 per month pension. He did not live to see its unraveling when the textile industry migrated to other countries, displacing thousands of workers. Nor did he see the South begin to reinvent itself though I believe he would have understood the need. When the construction of I-85 split his farmland in half, he adapted by leasing plots to billboard advertisers. After all, he had forged his own path and scraped together a new life through hard work, determination and plain good sense, essentials not only for a successful life, but a strong society. He was not one to stand still in the changing times.

Carl Jung said, "We are born in a certain time and a certain place, and like vintage wine we retain the flavor of our origins." So many flavors of my Southern origins overwhelm me when I inhale the pungent smell of hay while on a Halloween hayride with my granddaughters. I am transported straight away to my grandfather's farm. The acrid smell of smoke stings my eyes reminding me of the smokehouse, an outbuilding on the farm where bulky hams were hung to cure. Spilled gasoline and motor oil conjure up Grandpa's lean-to garage and his 1955 coral and shadow-grey Chevy. I can almost hear the mournful moo of cows in the pasture, the brittle cackle of hens in the coop and the grunting of hogs at the trough. And, of course, the tastes from my grandfather's land and animals hold strongest sway. Warm milk straight from the cow. Homemade livermush from a hog slaughtered in the dead of winter. Pillowy chicken and dumplings, greens slick with bacon drippings and jars of pear preserves with al dente pear pieces the size of your thumb.

I heave a nostalgic sigh for that simpler South, the mostly rural South when livelihoods were tangible—paid in bushels and pecks. But the mill has long since been razed. The fields fallow. Only 2% of the population are farmers. In their place, corporate banking, technology, pharmaceuticals, and tourism grow, becoming the New South. Progress.

In this new era our Southern culture, history, and heritage are regarded as old fashioned, if not embarrassing and in need of revision. Even Southern comfort food is cooked with a "twist" in upscale restaurants. My precious heritage was afforded me by my hardscrabble grandfather who embodied time-worn Southern values of dedication to family, love of the land, the honor of your handshake, and a desire to make a better way for those who came after him. I suffer no embarrassment.

The more the South changes, the more my grandfather's memory sharpens and digs deeper into my molecular makeup. Writer Julia Cameron hits close to clarifying why these images touch to the quick of me when she says, "Our ancestral wisdom lives on in our blood and in our bones." The South may change and reinvent itself, but the legacy of the people who defined my Southern heritage will proudly live on in me.•

Janice Luckey lives in Davidson, North Carolina, where she is a member of The Write Stuff sponsored by the Mooresville Public

One Southerner's Legacy

Library. Writing became a rhythm of her life when she self-published a summer romance novel in a three-ring binder in junior high school. This sparked a life-long love affair with all things bookish—writing, reading, books and libraries. Janice hopes to pass that love to her granddaughters by writing stories about those in our Southern heritage.

Dogwood Johnny
by Mary Alice Dixon

He might have been born up North, but Johnny became a Southerner the day he started looking for the Holy Grail. It was a hopeless cause—his Lost Cause—but he never lost hope.

It all began in 1961, when he was 50. That's when he accepted a job promotion and moved his family from Pennsylvania to North Carolina. Their new house, Johnny insisted, must be built "close enough to church so we can hear the Mass bells every day." His children lived in the vectors of his Catholic *feng shui*.

Johnny was a devout Catholic in the Protestant South and a brilliant engineer. In North Carolina, he once went to church for 700 days in a row. "Kept exact count," he remembered, with near-perfect mathematical recall.

From the backyard of the new house in Charlotte, across the field from St. Gabriel's, the bells of the church named for the messenger archangel spoke to Johnny in a way only he could hear. Thus, began his quest.

What ever happened to that Holy Grail? he pondered, then asked the same of family, friends, priests, even the dentist.

To find out what happened, I need to know what the Grail looks like, he reasoned, *so I know what I'm looking for.* The search for the Grail led him to angel wings. *How did angels fly while holding up the Grail?* Johnny figured the angels who carried the Ark of the Covenant in Exodus must be like the angels who lifted the Grail to catch Christ's blood at the Crucifixion. It was his own private mythology.

Ark research was added to Grail research. He went to the diocesan library, the synagogue library, the public library. *How big is an angel's wingspan? Do wings grow from torso or shoulders? Do they get in the way of an angel's arms?*

And feathers, he contemplated, *feathers are essential to your angel's aeronautical lift. How many feathers on the average angel wing?* Librarians had no answers.

He set out to discover the anatomy of angels through the miracle of engineering.

"If anybody can understand angel wings, it's me," he told them at the Charlotte Chapter of the Professional Engineers Club, of which he was a charter member. "After all, I'm the guy who got a patent for a fighter plane part in WWII. I'm your wingman with angels, fellas."

With a ruler, a compass, and a genius for calculus, Johnny made blueprints of angel wings, meticulously measured, neatly labeled.

He debated angel wings with a friend, Bob, a successful dentist who majored in engineering at Belmont Abbey College. Bob claimed, "God can make angels any damn way He wants; they don't have to obey your laws of physics."

Johnny offered Bob a shot of Irish Whiskey, then grinned. "Hell, Bob, you're a dentist, whadda you know?" They both laughed and took a sip. "And where's that Holy Grail?"

They sat in Johnny's kitchen, he in a white, short-sleeved shirt with a pen in his chest pocket, Brylcreem-black hair already shading to salt, round glasses half-way down his nose. Behind him the kitchen walls were papered in red parrots with three-inch yellow beaks, his wife's new wallpaper.

That morning Johnny's eyebrows rose at the parrot paper. "Looks like Elsie-the-Cow's housedress on Borden's Buttermilk," he said, winking. His wife hated buttermilk.

Johnny crowed, sounding more rooster than parrot, flapped elbow wings in mock horror. She laughed.

"Really, honey, your wallpaper's perfect," Johnny said. "Those parrot wings look awfully good."

"I knew you'd like the birds, dear," she answered.

Her smile was honeysuckle happy. She knew this crazy man, loved him deeply. He blew her three kisses and headed out to the yard to plant another dogwood in the Saturday morning sun. He dug deep in blood-red Carolina clay, feeding the dirt with wet coffee grounds from the kitchen percolator, giving the sapling its first wake-up call.

Dogwood Johnny

7

"Christ was crucified on the wood of a dogwood tree," he told the children. "The chalice that caught His blood, that was the Holy Grail. Carolina Dogwood, that was the Tree of the Angels."

He tended his dogwoods for 45 years. In his trees he put birdhouses. He studied bird wings in flight, angels in Renaissance paintings. His trees blossomed, smelling of Easter and sunrise, marked with the nails of the Passion on April-pink petals. "Dogwood Johnny," his kids called him, as he grew deep, old-fashioned roots in the booming New South. At 95, he still drew angel wings.

When Johnny died, a stranger bought the house, knocked it down, parrots and all. He cut down every last dogwood. But one grew back. Last time I saw it, a bird's nest sat in that tree. Now I'm the one watching for wings, searching for signs of Dad's Holy Grail. •

Mary Alice Dixon lives and writes in Charlotte, North Carolina. She is a former attorney who often served as court-appointed counsel in juvenile court. She has also been a professor of architectural history, teaching in Charlotte, Minneapolis, and China. She belongs to Charlotte Writers' Club and Charlotte Lit. Her recent writing is in, or forthcoming from, *Living Springs* and *Main Street Rag*. She volunteers with hospice and delights in reading poetry to the dying, grateful for the lesson this teaches about what really matters.

A Southern Girlhood—No Crinolines

by Annie McLeod Jenkins

I remember the air—dry and hot, heavy and still, full of the potential for sweat and discomfort. I remember the smell of the pine sap, the decaying under-layer of needles, the greenish smell of a nearby pond and hardwoods. I remember the freedom.

We were three skinny ten-year-old girls—Margaret, Kent, and Annie—still children in those days before ten-year-old girls were regularly wearing bras. We set out, looking for adventure, dressed in our high-top canvas tennis shoes (not "sneakers"), our boys' white t-shirts (called "undershirts" in that day), and our blue jeans (not just "jeans"). Our goal was at least a mile, maybe two, by road and probably three-quarters of a mile by the proverbial crow's flight. Our starting point was Margaret's home in the country, eighteen miles from my home in Winnsboro and about a mile from the nearest neighbors. Dauntless, we were kitted out with WWII Army surplus sleeping bags, canteens, knapsacks, assorted knives, and items we thought necessary to survive a couple of days camping alone in a South Carolina July.

The campsite we chose, down a sandy path behind tiny
New Hope ARP Church and near its ancient cemetery, was on
a slight knoll in a grove of longleaf pines. Nearby was a farm
pond, and we had the advantage of a nice little spring not too
far away. The place did catch an intermittent breeze. Whether
we considered that point at all in choosing, I do not recall.

The expedition lasted a mere three days and two nights.
During those 48 hours, particularly in the heat of each day,
we spent much of our time just poking around, no one to
bother us or to direct our activities. We collected firewood and
dug for fishing worms. We caught crickets, with their nasty
penchant for "spitting tobacco." We trekked the path to the
spring for our water, which from the source tasted leafy but
took on a metallic taste after sitting a while in our old canteens.
No matter. The trip to the spring called for bravery. It was hot;
the Johnson grass cut our bare legs; the underbrush was thick;
and we knew that copperheads lurked too-near water for our
liking on arid summer days. During the worst of the heated
day, we stripped to our underwear and sat in a line on our
sleeping bags, taking turns tickling each other's backs for the
cooling shiver.

In the late afternoon we fished with our cane poles, dangling
fat worms and the occasional cricket. Everyone knew this was
the best time of day for success. The one fish we caught—a
nice little bream—we scaled and gutted with my prized Roy
Rogers pocketknife. For breading our catch, we acquired some
cornmeal in a barter with Ella (of Sam and Ella, the couple
who lived in a little tenant house just down the sandy road),
using a can of SpaghettiOs in trade. Needing a way to heat our

iron skillet over the wood fire, we "borrowed" a broken headstone from the cemetery to use as a substitute grill. A debate arose whether this might be considered sacrilegious, but we decided God did want us to eat.

The second night brought the threat of a quintessential Southern thunderstorm, with distant thunder and lightning. We did not have a tent, and we knew that a grove of trees was not safe. I think we made an escape plan, maybe to run to Sam and Ella's porch. But we survived without a drenching and discovered the next morning—to our amazement—that Mr. Henry, Margaret's father, had spent the night in his truck, parked near the church, just in case we needed rescuing. To his credit, he never showed his face during the night nor suggested that we should come home with him.

Why, after six intervening decades, do I look back on these simple days and nights and see them so clearly? At the time, it was just another 48 hours of the "tomboy life" I lived with my friends. But now, from this vantage point on the other side of those 60 years, I understand the significance of three little girls—generally powerless—experiencing real freedom, facing obstacles, using their brains, not giving up, making decisions, tolerating discomfort, and eating a fish they caught, cleaned, and cooked all by their own skinny selves. We were as good as any boys.

And we knew it. •

Annie Jenkins lives in Winston-Salem, North Carolina. She declares, "My writing life consists of good intentions and some scattered notebooks. I've taken a few writing classes, written some pleasing (to me) poetic sketches of characters from my childhood, and published one essay in The Appalachian Trail magazine. But generally, I've never decided exactly where I want to aim my pen.

.

Great Aunt Dora
by Pam Brinegar

As I think back on the times, it was the lingering undertones that defined the kitchens of my youth. Grandmother Stella's place hinted of home-cured sausage and country ham. Granny Edna's smelled of pies, jam, and the grease drippings jar. And, Great Aunt Dora's house offered up a combined fragrance of fried Spam and rust. She and her house were special for many reasons as I remember. Granny Edna and I visited Dora in her mountain home every summer.

Short and ample, Dora struggled to retain her youthfulness with upswept hair and a tightly laced waist. She adopted 1920's rolled stockings, avoiding the once stylish below-the-knee spot by sliding her elasticized bands thigh high. Leaning forward on tiptoe to turn the generator crank on her oak telephone while yelling, "Hello, central, hello," she looked just like an old-fashioned Gibson Girl.

In her spartan kitchen, an oilcloth-covered table held a Pick-a-Prayer box, the latest Upper Room, a Bible, butter dish, jelly jar, and a small woodpecker balanced over a hollowed log containing toothpicks. When pushed down, the bird's pot metal beak picked up the small slivers of wood that Dora threw away after I played with them. Polite people, she declared, did not ever put toothpicks in their mouths.

Dora's Sunday dinners featured applesauce, Jell-O, and thinly-sliced fried Spam, a combination she offered up for every meal until we emptied the tin of potted pork. Her most useful culinary accomplishment, however, involved wielding a dull table knife to make strategic cuts in hot dogs and bologna slices. Slit just right, they would not curl when heated in the cast iron pan she kept scrubbed clean with powdered cleanser. I certainly believed the whispered story that Dora's late husband took all his meals at the once nearby Hotel Delaney.

A porcelain sink, indelibly rust-stained by running water deemed unusable for drinking or cooking, stood beneath the kitchen's empty window ledge. Knotted rope hung over a nearby hook, looping through the outside wall and draping through two hundred feet of trees before ending, tied to a dirty cowbell on neighbor Emil's cabin porch. When she rang the bell, Emil ambled to Dora's house and carried out whatever task had crossed her mind at the time. Rarely did she call on him in emergencies. For those, Dora pulled a heavy pistol from under her pillow and took charge herself.

Dora looked like the wealthiest person in those parts, neighbor Emil among the poorest. For his meals, he enjoyed fried chicken or squirrel along with fruits and vegetables grown in his own hillside backyard. He kept fresh cow's milk in Mason jars under a small waterfall. He ate onions the way I did apples, and he cared for his cast iron pans by wiping them down with plenty of grease.

On rainy days, for my health, Dora handed me one prophy-lactic Luden's menthol cough drop. Sometimes, she let me walk across a wooden bridge to Richardson's Store and buy a Nesbitt's orange-flavored soft drink. Coca-Cola represented danger—she believed it still contained cocaine. Mr. Richardson, who was the sheriff, barber, grocer, and postmaster, wore a silver star pinned on a sleeveless ribbed cotton undershirt and chewed a huge tobacco wad. He stopped talking only long enough to spit. I never understood a word he uttered.

Iron-red streaks also marred the porcelain in Dora's bathroom, a place that became one of ghostly terror to my mind. I often sneaked onto the porch after dark to overhear the stories they told. Through the creaking rhythm of porch rocking chairs, I learned a lot about dead folks, including those two awe-inspiring—yet clearly inadequate life companions—their doctor husbands. I also learned that Dora believed a sign from beyond marked every person's death. These manifestations assumed many forms—a pack of howling wild dogs entering a yard or strange lights floating around a darkened sickroom wall. I dismissed all of that stuff outright because it was obvious Edna disbelieved it.

When I was about five years old, I overheard one startling reminiscence. Edna and Dora recalled how a few years earlier the local undertaker had embalmed Dora's husband in his home bathtub. That was a common enough practice of the

Great Aunt Dora

era, but one certainly unfamiliar to me. "We never could clean up all that blood," I heard Edna say.

Eavesdropping from underneath a window standing open to the scene of this dreadful event, I struggled to remain quiet. Those iron-red bathtub stains surely resulted from something far worse than the kitchen sink rust. That open window provided the only way back inside without my being discovered. Creeping over its sill cautiously, I closed my eyes and raced past the terrifying tub and toward the comforting aromas of fried Spam and rust. •

Pam Brinegar is a Lexington, Kentucky, family historian whose articles have appeared in various publications including *NGS Magazine*, *Kentucky Ancestors*, *Bluegrass Roots*, and *Ohio Genealogical Society Quarterly*. Her favorite current project centers on an attorney/educator/Episcopal priest turned Kentucky circuit court judge-imposter who fled Boston in 1909 to escape charges of forgery, larceny, and bigamy.

Southern Tides
by Landis Wade

When I think of the South, I think of Wrightsville Beach, where warm waves lap up on miles of white sand separated from the North Carolina mainland by Harbor Island and the Intracoastal Waterway. And when I think of the beach, I think of my dad, a Southern gentleman to the end, and my great-grandmother, whom we called Bama, a genteel Southern lady who decided to become a Wrightsville Beach businesswoman in her 60s when husband Bumpy "hit the road." And because it was too risky in the 1930s South for a bank to loan money to a woman for a business enterprise, family lore is that Bama recruited a well-connected male politician to co-sign the loan she needed to build her hotel.

The South is keen on family and so was Bama. She thought of her guests as next-of-kin. She loved treating them to "three hots and a flop" and telling them stories on her ocean-front porch with the waves as back-up. While planning the hotel, she decided to run a small rooming house at the beach, and as my dad liked to tell the story, she was "over the moon" when she called Charlotte, saying, "I got the Kitty." Those four words became a family metaphor for the perfect real estate acquisition. Sixty years later, when my wife and I bought a small cabin in the North Carolina mountains, I called Dad and said simply, "I got the Kitty."

After "the Kitty," Bama built her hotel. It had wood siding, with three floors, long open air porches, a wooden bridge on the main level that led to a cabana on the beach, panoramic views of the beach, and a big sign on top that faced sound-side saying, "The Landis." Before the hotel got battered and bruised by Hurricane Hazel, my dad was a hotel lifeguard in the 1940s and early 50s during his high school and college years. He waited tables and saved pretty girls who pretended to be in distress from swimming too close to the jetties.

Dad spent his entire life in the South and at least three-tenths of it at Wrightsville Beach. He never wanted to vacation anywhere else. We joked in his later years that if he ever went to Myrtle Beach, the credit card company would cancel his card, thinking an imposter had stolen it. And so it was, that with every summer vacation we took when I was a child, our family piled into the station wagon to head to Wrightsville Beach. And Dad always sang, "Hi-ho, hi-ho, it's off to the beach we go." I did the same with my kids when we went to Wrightsville Beach.

Bama's relatives stayed in "The Out-Landis," a basic structure Bama built behind the hotel to keep the family from scaring off the guests. Bama served meals family style with a Southern touch—a staple and two vegetables plus desert. She had a cook and a handy man, but Bama was the matriarch in charge. If I did an errand, I might get a nickel for a coke at the soda shack next door, where I could search in the sand under the floorboards for more nickels. Bama was the reason Wrightsville Beach became our ancestral beach.

As a child, it felt like infinity to get from Charlotte to the beach, but the pay-off was always grand. When we reached the drawbridge, we'd roll down the windows, suck in that sweet, salt air and know that the fun was about to begin. Dad smiled more at Wrightsville Beach than anywhere else, and in his last days, when dementia took over and the end was near, an attending Charlotte doctor asked, "Do you know where you are?" and Dad said with absolute certainty, "Wrightsville Beach."

Bama's death in her late 90s put an end to The Landis, but not an end to the family's appreciation for what she started. Over the years, I've had more relatives living at or visiting Wrightsville Beach than no-see-ems on Sand Dollar Island. And it never mattered where we stayed, or how hot the sun, because Wrightsville Beach was like being in the shade of our family tree. I liked the stories about Great-Uncle Frank the best, who everyone called Red because of his flaming hair. He was Bama's ne'er-do-well son, who attended State college, joined the Navy, settled in a trailer near the beach, divorced his wife because she didn't like his dogs and told Bama he refused to be buried in the family plot in Charlotte because the ride was way too long for him.

According to the compass, Wrightsville Beach is due east of Charlotte. But my heart tells me it is due South, where life and memories ebb and flow on Southern Tides. •

Southern Tides

Landis Wade is a recovering trial lawyer, award-winning author and host of Charlotte Readers Podcast, where local and regional authors give voice to their written words. His third book—*The Christmas Redemption*—won the Holiday category of the 12th Annual National Indie Excellence Awards. His essays, "Shelby" and "Two Good Swings," appeared in *Bearing Up* and *Exploring*, two earlier anthologies of the Personal Story Publishing Project.

Southern Lineage
by Grace Ellis

My mother was groomed to be deeply Southern. Not "Dukes of Hazard" Southern (Heaven forbid!) but aristocratic Charleston/Savannah Southern. Her father's grandfather was one of the secretaries of the treasury for the Confederacy, and his mansion later became the site of Ashley Hall, a private school for Charleston's privileged young women. Her mother's grandfather was a distinguished Presbyterian minister, and her mother's first cousin married Woodrow Wilson.

When I took a course in Asian theater, the professor commented that I had an unusually good understanding of the caste system. Of course I did. My mother's family considered themselves to be members of the "professional" class— doctors, lawyers, professors, ministers, and maybe bankers, too. They looked down on "working class" people—and also, to an extent, on entrepreneurs, whose wealth exceeded theirs, but who were considered to be crude. And, of course, in that era, African Americans were seen as an altogether separate category. My mother's mother taught her there were two types of behavior—what was "proper" and what was "common," a word that meant not "frequently occurring" but "an indication of being a lower caste commoner."

As she grew up, my mother rebelled against her upbringing. Although she was eligible to make her debut at the St. Cecilia Society ball, she declined because she did not like associating with those snooty young women. In college, my mother was active in the YWCA and attended a conference where young, black and white women ate meals at the same table. The story goes that after this occasion, FBI agents visited her father to apprise him of her misconduct. Although my grandfather undoubtedly disapproved of her behavior, he disapproved even more of the government poking its nose into his business. He sent them packing.

After college during World War II, my mother worked for the Red Cross, visiting black residents of the coastal islands near Charleston, where she conversed with them in the creole language known as Gullah. She supported their efforts to make financial contributions to the Red Cross, upsetting the white women of Charleston, who wanted to see themselves as the wealthy elite and the black women as the poor who depended on them.

My mother fell in love with a young man with a deep interest in social justice, who was headed for seminary. (On their first date, she berated him for belonging to a fraternity.) My parents were married at the end of August in 1944. Her mother urged them to postpone the ceremony for a few days—into September—because a marriage in the heat of August implied improper haste.

I was born eighteen months after their August wedding. Sixteen months later my brother James came along, and finally twins—four of us under five. My mother was embarrassed to have so many children so close together, something her mother would have labeled as "common."

Taking care of four children and the household was a full-time job. Mother had only one day off each week, when a babysitter came to watch us, and she and my father went to Warrenton or Manassas, where he visited parishioners in the hospital, and she went shopping for groceries. She had learned to cook from my father's mother, to whom she became very close. (Her own mother knew only three recipes for fancy desserts because "the help" did all the cooking.) Throughout our childhood, our mother cooked three meals a day, every day, even on vacations.

But after we had all entered school, she began to defy the Southern notions of a woman's proper role by applying her administrative skills to various part-time and volunteer jobs. Over the years, she established the first Alumni Association at Stillman College in Tuscaloosa; worked for a publication called *The Review and Expositor* in Louisville, Kentucky; helped to establish a pre-school at Louisville Seminary; re-organized a church library in Richmond, Virginia; worked at Alternatives for Simpler Living, in Atlanta, producing booklets encouraging simpler lifestyles; and oversaw and edited a recipe book for healthier, more planet-friendly church dinners. Her mother would not have approved.

In spite of all the ways she had rejected her upbringing, Mother was not completely free of its restrictions. She retained the beliefs—learned from her parents—that there is a right way to do everything, that it is important to follow the rules, that we should never disappoint others. She was rarely playful or exuberant. When she played the piano, she kept the tempo as steadily as a metronome, no flourishes. When she cooked, she followed the recipe to the letter. All her four children have found ways to rebel against this strict regimen. But freeing ourselves is hard. After all, those rules are an indelible part of our Southern lineage. •

Grace Ellis is a playwright, poet, and author of creative nonfiction living in Winston-Salem. She has participated in Winston-Salem Writers' open mic nights and Poetry in Plain Sight. She also moderates the Winston-Salem Writers Script Group. She has seen dozens of her plays performed—many at the Greensboro Playwrights Forum Evenings of Short Plays. In 2020 she plans to teach a playwriting class at The Little Theater of Winston-Salem and to help residents at Arbor Acres and Salemtown to devise their own plays.

Sufis in Florida

by Fatima Alharthi

A few years after September 11, 2001, my cousin came to Boston to earn her bachelor's degree. She was consistent in telling everyone she was from Lebanon. "There is no way I would tell them I am from Saudi Arabia, especially not taxi drivers," she said.

I never knew how to dress up facts in a lie, how to hide my identity in a "fancy turban," which is an idiom we use in my homeland where we do not wear turbans, just other practical and distinctively cultural head coverings. And so, whenever I traveled, either for leisure or study, I would answer that question truthfully.

"What brings you to Tallahassee?" asked the first Arab woman I met in Florida as she served me stuffed grape leaves. "Florida State," I answered to her only while enduring from others around us their piercing stares at my hijab.

"You are experiencing the prejudice of the South," reflected my critical-theory professor after I shared with him about my encounters. With his words, I envisioned "the South" back home, the remote, peculiar South where apes invade hotel chalets, and misty mountains offer temporary relief from the kingdom's sultry summer, where unveiling a woman's face would be like walking naked on Tallahassee's Gaines Street, where my relative divorced her husband because his tenure-track teaching job did not make her feel welcomed among those southern Saudis.

But for me, experiencing America's South is helping validate who I am. In fall 2019, I started teaching Middle Eastern literature in translation. On the day memorializing 9/11, we began with a moment of silent remembrance. As a practicing Sufi, I recited to myself Quran verses about love and mercy. I mourned the loss 18 years earlier of 3,000 innocent souls taken in a horrific, murderous calamity. I acknowledged that the tension between Saudis and Americans began to fracture from the imprudence of a selfish, radical, anti-Islamic terrorist mentality, such thinking at great odds with true Muslims and that of us Sufis specifically.

My American students and I agreed on how hard it is for one to become a true Sufi. For us, Sufism is about spreading internal and external peace, not just whirling dervishes and ecstatic dance. Sufism is about mindfulness. My students' understanding of Sufism had evolved during discussions of novels such as Elif Shafak's *Forty Rules of Love*, Tahar Ben Jelloun's *This Blinding Absence of Light*, and the biography of the ninth century mystic Mansour al-Hallaj. Some of the descriptions touched on refraining from inflicting harm on one's self, fellow humans, and non-humans. Others described Sufism as observing God in every action, submission to life's occurrences, and avoiding violence.

We humans don't choose our genes, our places of birth, dialects, and appearances. They choose us, and sometimes also do the places we work, live, or in my case, study and teach. When Florida State chose me, I yielded, not because I didn't have other educational chances in the Northeast, I did. I yielded because I believe I was destined to interact with the people and places on a part of the earth so distinct from other places I have been such as New York, San Francisco, Europe, and Australia. In Florida, anxiety is a lizard, a frog, an alligator, a thunderstorm, and a power outage during 90-degree days after a damaging hurricane. For me, anxiety in Florida is also a piercing stare and a racist remark. Anxiety is a hesitation to communicate and assumptions made on appearances. But for me as a Sufi, submission—acceptance—releases anxiety and brings bliss.

Sufism taught me to submit to body scans in airports, to endure the huffs, and the "you don't understand anything" remark of a nurse unable to convert my weight and height given her in kilos and centimeters. Sufism taught me to accept stern glares, to forgive sexual harassment, and to move forward. But on occasion, fear did stop me from practicing my driving lessons or from walking to the campus' library all because a Southerner driving by had rolled down his window and shouted profanities at me. Another time, a Christian missionary shouted at me, "Forsake your false god. Forsake Muhammad."

But I remember also my leisurely walk in New York's Central Park, and a runner cursing my God. I remember the obscenities yelled at me by the Australian lady in Sydney's downtown, and I realize that prejudice is not unique to the South. Prejudice resides in every person. Prejudice is the plight of the human ego. We each have one and we are each challenged to rise above it, each in our own way. My path begins with thoughts of love and mercy. •

Fatima Alharthi was born in Dammam, Saudi Arabia. She is a graduate assistant at Florida State University where she studies for a PhD in Creative Writing. She wrote previously under Fatima Jamal. Her fiction can be found on *Smokelong Quarterly*, *Apeiron Review*, *Flyleaf Journal*, and *Santa Ana River Review* among others. Fatima believes in writing to bridge the gap between the East and the West. She currently lives in Tallahassee with her husband and three children.

How Uncle Gene Got His Cut
by Richard Groves

To get to the roots of my family's squabble over money you have to go back more than one hundred years to the turn of the twentieth century. That's when Fred and Catharine Cook, my grandparents on my mother's side, traveled by wagon from Missouri to North Louisiana where they bought a quarter section of land, 160 acres. There they built an impressive house, which unfortunately burned to the ground and was replaced by one not nearly so grand.

It was subsistence farming. My grandfather rarely made money (occasionally he sold a little cotton). Mostly the family—which grew to include ten children—got by on the vegetables they grew and the animals—cows, pigs, and chickens—they raised.

The family survived the Depression that way and sent four boys into the service in World War II. They all came back; Gene, the youngest, had a scar in his side from a bullet wound he received in the Philippines.

Catherine died in 1930. Fred lived into his 90s and died when I was in college. One by one the children grew up, got married and left the farm for jobs in the city, leaving the home place desolate and in shabby disrepair.

Almost unnoticed, the nearby city of Shreveport had been growing throughout the 20th century, annexing its way southward toward the abandoned family farm. By the time the family realized it, the city limit was on the other side of the property, and my aunts and uncles were looking at paying taxes on 160 acres. It was time to sell off Fred and Catharine's dream.

It was done piecemeal. First, some of the woods where I played as a boy were sold to make way for the new loop around the city. The rest of the woods were sold to the developers of the South Park Mall. Finally, only one piece of land was left—a pasture that extended from the house where I grew up to the intersection of the Meriwether and Jewella roads. And there was a potential buyer.

The brothers and sisters—all ten of them—gathered in an attorney's office to hear the final offer: five-and-a-half million dollars. Jaws dropped all round the table. None of the siblings had gone to college. Most of the brothers worked for the local gas company. In their lives, they had never dreamed of that much money.

"Well," one of the brothers said when he gathered his wits about him, "it won't be hard to figure each share: just divide five-and-a-half million by ten. Five-hundred-and-fifty thousand dollars each."

That's when Uncle Joe from Mississippi spoke up. "We all know it's nine, not ten, don't we?"

He had just broken a decades old silence, saying out loud what everyone knew but no one talked about: that Uncle Gene was not the child of my grandparents; he was the out-of-wedlock son of my Aunt Florence, the oldest girl in the family. Marriage had been out of the question and giving the baby up for adoption was unthinkable for a poor farm family in the 1920's. So, my granddad had said he would take the child in and raise him as his own, which is what he did. As to what people might think, he said, "It ain't none of their business."

The family sat in stunned silence. Gene was there at the table.

Finally, my mother—bless her heart—spoke.

> Here's all you need to know about my mother. One day, decades later, when her pastor came to visit her in the nursing home, he found her in her wheelchair with her chin resting on her chest.
>
> "Mrs. Groves," he said. "Are you asleep?"
>
> "No," she said, barely looking up. "I thought if I closed my eyes you would think I was and leave me alone. Obviously, it didn't work."
>
> That was my mom.

"Joe," she said, "I'm sure that legally speaking you're right. And if you insist, we'll divide the money nine ways and leave Gene out. But then, the rest of us are going to re-pool our shares and re-divide it and give Gene a cut. And then," she paused for maximum impact, "no one in this family will speak to you for the rest of your sorry life."

Uncle Joe looked across the table at my mother's set jaw and cold stare.

"Well," he conceded weakly, "Dad did raise him as one of the boys."

My mother said she was 22 years old when she found out that Gene was her nephew, not her brother. I was middle-aged when I learned that my war hero, the man I thought was my uncle, was really my cousin. Not that it mattered. I called him Uncle Gene till the day he died. •

Dr. Richard Groves is a retired minister and educator. He has taught in departments of religion and philosophy at Tufts University, Wake Forest University, Salem College, and High Point University. He is the editor of a book of speeches by William Louis Poteat, early 20th century president of Wake Forest University (published by Wake Forest University, and two 17th century works on religious liberty, including *The Bloody Tenent of Persecution* by Roger Williams (both published by Mercer University Press). He writes regular opinion pieces for the Winston-Salem Journal.

Forgetting the Smilings
by Joel Stegall

Well-known, of course, is that during the Jim Crow era Southern states maintained separate public schools for white and for African-American children.

Robeson County, North Carolina, where my family lived in the mid-1950s, had not two but four public school systems. Besides schools for whites and blacks, the county had two other segregated school districts—one for Lumbee Indians and one for Smilings.

I attended one of the county's white high schools. Like many teenagers, I took part-time jobs so I could have my own spending money. I worked in tobacco fields, pumped gas, and clerked in a clothing store—all jobs in which I met people of all races throughout the community. I also drove a school bus carrying 30 white kids every school day over the same roads used by buses from African-American, Lumbee, and Smilings schools.

My most interesting teenager job was measuring tobacco crop

land for the Department of Agriculture to help maintain price stability in the tobacco market. (Yes, at age 17, before I needed to shave more than once a week, I was a federal agent.) The job took me to farms run by whites, blacks, Indians, and Smilings. Spending time with these people where they lived and worked, I soon realized I knew little about how we all came to be there. Of course, I had read about my ancestors, the European colonists. And I was aware the black farmers I met were grandchildren of enslaved people. But the Lumbees and the Smilings were a mystery.

Years afterward, I learned it likely the Lumbee Indians were descendants of the Lost Colonists who intermarried with Native Americans and moved inland, perhaps in the latter 1600s. Still later and after escaping President Jackson's Indian Removal efforts of the 1830s, Lumbees were pressed into labor during the Civil War to build earth fortifications on the Cape Fear River at Fort Fisher. Some may have worked alongside my great-grandfather. Lumbees who resisted forced labor slipped into the swamps, as did the Lowry family. This band of Lumbee "outlaws and bandits" fought against the Confederate Home Guard. The famous Henry Lowry was pursued for six years with a bounty on his head, but he avoided capture and disappeared.

But what about the Smilings?

Around 1900, several families with white, African-American, and Indian ancestries moved into Robeson County from South Carolina. Back there, they had been known as "Red Bones." Claiming a common racial heritage with Robeson's Lumbees, the new arrivals attempted to enroll their children in Indian schools. But Indian school officials refused, saying they were not "real" Indians. The immigrant families—one named Smiling—sued. That name stuck through the court proceedings.

The North Carolina Supreme Court ruled in 1915 that the Smilings were at least part Indian, and that their children were entitled to attend Lumbee Indian schools. When the Indians still refused to accept them, Robeson County set up a fourth school district for the Smilings.

Forty years after the four school districts were set in place in Robeson County, I was measuring tobacco crop land there. The most memorable experience was on a farm operated by a Smiling sharecropper. The farmer was a friendly sort, and we chatted amicably as we walked his tobacco field. He told me with obvious pride that his young teenage son did well in school and wanted to go to Pembroke State College. At that time, I did not know many details of the Smilings' story, but I knew enough to recognize that this was likely the first time ever that such an ambition could have been imaginable for him and his people. I felt honored he would share this dream with me.

When schools were integrated in the 1960s, the Smilings no longer had a reason for separate status. They had become an identifiable ethnic group only a half-century earlier and only in their legal pursuit to provide education for their children. Accordingly, census reports of later years include the Smilings under "Some Other Race," or "Two or More Races." Indeed, the Smilings have ceased to exist as a separate, identifiable group; that status is most likely what they always wanted.

Most compelling for me is the memory of that Smilings tenant farmer telling me he was so proud his son might finish high school and go to college, something the father could never have dreamed of doing. I wonder what that farmer's son is doing now? I wonder if his grandchildren are aware that their granddaddy was one of the Smilings.

Do they even know who the Smilings were? •

In Joel Stegall's childhood home, words were valued. His father was a preacher; his mother a storyteller and frustrated writer. At Wake Forest University, Joel wandered into a forgettable assignment as managing editor of the school paper. In his career as a professor and academic administrator, he wrote too many tedious memos and inconsequential academic papers. Since retiring, he spends an inordinate amount of time searching for his writer's voice, hoping occasionally to do something others want to read.

The Great Dumpling Divide
by Susan Griner

M y 13-year-old daughter Marie and I had different reasons to worry about our trip to Tennessee from Seattle. Hers had to do with chiggers, ticks, and poisonous snakes. Mine had to do with returning to a place where I'd never felt accepted. We agreed on one thing though—we were looking forward to seeing Marie's second cousin, Delilah. She'd turned 2 and we had yet to meet her. My cousin-in-law, Cora, and her husband, Jackson, picked us up from the Nashville airport and took us to the Cracker Barrel restaurant in the small, nearby town of Lebanon. I told Marie about the stick candy and trinkets in the store to distract her from the looks she might get.

When we walked through the door it was like going through a portal in time.

"So many Q-tips," Marie whispered to me.

So many "white people" of all ages. And now one Japanese-American woman and one Chinese teenager were among them.

We were greeted with some polite smiles, and a few children gawked. I hadn't told Marie we might stand out here. She was used to a diverse West Coast community where she blended in. Of course, she had heard my stories of being taunted for my "slanty eyes" when I was growing up in Tennessee. I had told her that people were more accepting by the time I grew up— or they knew to keep it to themselves if they weren't. Marie was too busy staring at jawbreakers to notice anyone staring at her. Perhaps I was wary for nothing.

Marie's second cousin, Delilah, rushed to see her grandparents, Cora and Jackson, at the table where we were seated. Delilah's mom, Paige, caught up and gave us hard hugs. Three generations sat around the table, studying Marie and me. The child we'd come to see had brown hair that spiraled around her face and a toddler tummy. Marie finally won her over with a "magic" quarter.

A waitress with hair piled high came by and asked, "What are y'all feeling like today?"

Orders for dumplings were called out, so Marie ordered the same before I could stop her.

Before long the waitress set a platter of chicken and square dumplings in front of Marie.
"OMG! What's this?" Marie asked.

Cora gave her the "stink eye" for her language while I explained to everyone. "Marie was expecting Chinese dumplings."

THAT SOUTHERN THING

She pushed the plate away. "Is this Southern food?"

Jackson, a beanpole, nodded and polished them off.

Those were not the dumplings I remembered either. My Mom's were like melting clouds. She may have been Japanese, she but had adapted in many ways.

We stayed at Cora and Jackson's, and for a while Marie was thrilled to play with the dogs and with Delilah when she came over. Later, Marie complained when she wasn't allowed to swat a mosquito which is one of God's creatures according to Cora, who apparently hasn't heard of West Nile virus.

Marie and I made an outing to Ralph's donuts where I had met Marie's dad when we were in college. The donut shop hadn't changed much, except Ralph was gone. He was known for being snappy if you didn't know your order. He'd been replaced by a waitress in a hoodie. At the counter were two old men, one with a veteran's cap on. We sat at a counter the farthest away from them.

"What can I get you for?" the waitress asked.

"A chocolate covered, a lemon filled, and a Coke."

The waitress popped the bottle open and handed it to Marie. "That's free."

After we ate, I decided to get a box of donuts for our host family. I meant to get half a dozen, but I thought I heard the waitress say I could get 16 for two more dollars. Her accent was so heavy I couldn't be sure how many she meant so I picked out donuts until she called it good and closed the box. As we left, I wondered why the waitress gave Marie a free drink. Was it because she's cute or because she's Asian? Were those two old men staring at us because we were different or because Marie had chocolate on her nose and because my shirt was sprinkled with powdered sugar? I was wary where my daughter was not.

I'd like my daughter's memories of the South to be unaffected by my own. Marie might worry about biting or poisonous creatures on her visits and she might be annoyed by the hints from Cora that she needs "saving," but she will remember being with cousins, chasing fireflies, and eating banana pudding too. I need to remember those things as well, because we make our life memories from what we choose to see. •

Susan Griner is a Japanese-American author of children's fiction. Her work has been published in Babybug and Cricket magazines. She has also published two middle grade novels, *The Cemetery Sleeper*, an Appalachian ghost story and *Shy Ways*. She enjoys visiting schools and encouraging students to write. She lives in the Seattle area with her husband and two daughters.

How Do You Pronounce Ightham?
by Hugh Dussek, Ph.D.

Although I have lived in Charlotte, North Carolina, for many years, I retain a distinct British accent. If asked where I am from, I often respond that I am from the South—the south of London.

My childhood home on the edge of the southeast London suburbs overlooked a common. On pleasant days, I could head out for a ramble across the Kentish countryside—an area known as the "Garden of England." In Britain, you can set off on a whim and follow a network of ancient footpaths to look at old duck ponds and little country churches, half-timbered Tudor and Elizabethan houses, thatched cottages, and the remains of the activities of ancient dwellers and the Romans. The Romans left plenty of examples of their empire-building all over Britain—old forts, villas and bits of walls. Some of the medieval village churches have been there for over a thousand years. Their dusty monuments from long ago emanating the air of the lives of countless noble and laboring families. The confident Victorians left their mark with railways and sturdy brickwork and ironwork. Sometimes, I would get completely lost on one of these walks, but my trusty Ordnance Survey

How Do You Pronounce Ightham?

map always got me back on track. The British countryside breathes history. It is there, just below the surface of our modern world with its cars, technology, and preoccupations. Random walks in the countryside don't work particularly well in the South of the United States—the distances are too far, you can't just walk all over people's property, and it's hot.

Charlotteans like to grumble about the traffic, the woes of travelling on Interstate 77, or losing your way in the "Bermuda Triangle" of the Queens Road vortex. Traffic in Charlotte pales in comparison, however, to the South Circular in London. If you happen to live outside of London, you wouldn't dream of trying to drive into London. Driving in Britain is only for the brave. The roads are crowded, and, of course, it is all on the other side—the wrong side—of the road. Instead of the very practical American stop light, we British have a multi-lane adventure of fear known as the roundabout. Do you stop or do you go? Everyone else seems to know what's going on.

We still use the old Roman roads in Britain. They have been resurfaced a few times, but the Romans built roads straight from town to town. Many of our British roads are teeny-tiny and wind drowsily from village to village between tall hedgerows—practical in the days of an occasional hay cart, but a nightmare for today's drivers. What with jet lag and the illogical British fixation that any good car must have a manual gearbox (that is, a manual transmission), I advise you to avoid driving in Britain; we have very good trains.

Some roads in Charlotte have vaguely British-sounding names. These Americanized names don't always sound quite right to the British ear—such as Dovershire Road. Dover is a port in Kent, and the country is made up of shires, but I can't find a place called Dovershire in the United Kingdom. Maybe there was at one time, but it sounds odd. Indeed, the correct pronunciation of British place names is a trip into a minefield of quirkiness. Place names follow their own rules. For example, the town of Westerham is not called "wester-ham," but "west-ram," and the village of Ightham is not pronounced "igg-tham," but "eye-tem."

Names often reflect their historical roots. A name ending in "chester" indicates that it was a Roman town, and a name ending in "ton" or "ham" reflects a Saxon origin. It is interesting to think that the name bequeathed to a spot in Britain by a medieval knight or noble now adorns a place in the United States. What is this preoccupation with adopting British names for roads in Charlotte? There are plenty of good, solid American names such as Washington Avenue, rational names such as Main Street or Fifth Street, and roads named after prominent local families, such as Alexander Street and Davidson Street. There must be some practical reason for adopting British-sounding names. Perhaps they impart an aura of romance and charm emanating from the Britain of long ago. Runnymede Lane conjures up images of King John facing off against the barons and affixing his royal seal to the Magna Carta. Queens Road must be a majestic royal road. Even Dovershire Road sounds a nicer place than Fifth Street.

Although Merry England may be a long way away, Charlotte

How Do You Pronounce Ightham?

has a vaguely British resonance. I feel quite at home. It's hotter than London, but the roads are a lot better. •

Originally from London, England, Hugh Dussek has lived in Charlotte, North Carolina, for over twenty years. Hugh holds a doctoral degree in history from Union Institute & University in Cincinnati, Ohio, and is a professor at Central Piedmont in Charlotte, where he teaches courses on world civilizations and American history. Hugh serves on the Board of Trustees for The Charlotte Museum of History and gives presentations in the community and on television about American, British, and local history.

It's More Than a Drawl, Y'all
by Ken Chamlee

Rugged mountains and a creative writing program lured me to Colorado in my mid-twenties, and when I started graduate school in Fort Collins it was the first time I had ever lived outside of the South. It didn't take long for some distinctions to be made. After the first workshop a guy with a bushy mustache said,

"Nice poem, Tex."

"I'm not from Texas. I'm from South Carolina."

"Don't matter. Sounds the same."

I laughed, but thought it strange, because my only time in Texas had been driving I-40 across the panhandle on the way to the Grand Canyon a few years earlier. When I thought of Texas I thought of dust, cattle, the Two-Step, driving 150 miles to the store, longneck beers and barbeque without vinegar. I didn't think of magnolias or moonshine or Myrtle Beach.

I realized later that my fellow poet had probably not been in either state, much less in the South I knew. He was responding to a perception that all Southerners speak alike and had heard enough in my Upstate accent to convince him I was turning *ice* into *eyes* and pushing every diphthong over a three-syllable cascade. I didn't talk like that, though I was hearing differences in my voice and the voices of students I met from Greeley and Cheyenne. But you get used to what you hear, and soon I couldn't make any distinction between my voice and those of my Western compadres.

As no one in my immediate family had lived away from the Carolinas, I was an exotic. So, during that first year, before any of them came out to see me, I sent home boxes of slides to run through their carousel projector, complete with cassette-recorded narration and slide changes indicated by dinging a spoon on a juice glass. I introduced them to Rocky Mountain National Park, took them up Trail Ridge Road to Forest Canyon Overlook and Fall River Pass. I told them about bugling elk in Horseshoe Park and blue columbine in the high meadows.

A few weeks later I got a return package with some slides of their Pisgah hikes and family meals, narrated by my older brother. Good Lord! I thought. That can't be him; he sounds so Southern! What's happened to him? I flipped the cassette tape over to play the side I had recorded for them, and to my utter shock, I sounded just like my brother!

The ear deceives and the mind believes. I thought my workshop buddy tone deaf because he couldn't tell Lubbock from Laurens, but apparently, I couldn't either! I had gotten used to the Colorado cadence I was hearing daily and thought I was speaking it too.

Now neither my brother nor I have the tonal neutrality of a
Midwestern news anchor, nor do we have the languorous lilt
you hear in Charleston or Mobile. We speak from one pool of
the great linguistic lake that is "Southern," spreading from
Texas to the Tidewater, and it is not all the same, of course,
but delightfully varied by nuance, inflection, and pacing.

Listening carefully, to others as well as to oneself, will help us
remember that homogenous is a good label for milk, but a bad
brand for language. •

Kenneth Chamlee taught English at Brevard College for 40 years.
His poems have appeared in *The North Carolina Literary Review*, *Cold
Mountain Review*, *Ekphrasis*, and many others, including six editions of
Kakalak, An Anthology of Carolina Poets. He has received three
Pushcart Prize nominations and regularly teaches for the Great
Smokies Writing Program at UNC-Asheville. Ken lives in Mills
River, North Carolina, and is currently working on a poetic
biography of 19th-century American landscape painter Albert
Bierstadt. Check it out at www.kennethchamlee.com.

It's More Than a Drawl, Y'all

THAT SOUTHERN THING

48

This story includes explicit language and racial epithets.

All That I Could Say
by Lauren Summers

The first time was on a field trip at age twelve,
I was seated on the back of the bus. The memory so
clear to me as if it were yesterday—except it
wasn't and yet
occurrences such as these happen every day.

Dressed in Carhartt and washed denim jeans he turned around
and his blue-eyed stare preyed upon
me unprovoked as he finally opened his mouth to say,
"You're a niglet."
I inquired because at the time I had no clue what such a word
meant until he fixed his mouth to say,
"It means you're a tiny nigger."
At that moment it should've clicked
but the experience settled into my mind marred by the bliss of
not knowing
until a time would come where it would be defined.

Fifteen years old at my high school's football game, I stood in
the freezing weather atop a hill
watching the field, oblivious of the position I was soon to be
in until a white boy walked up to me
with a smirk on his face.
"Hey, my favorite nigger,"—Everything went silent except for

All That I Could Say

the sound of my heart that pounded
in my ears. I stood isolated inside that moment as his pink lips
kept moving and all I could see was
his dirty blonde hair,
his heavy stare,
the pattern on his coat,
his thick brown boots,
which I imagined stomping into my stomach. That's quite how
that moment felt, but like the careful
young black girl I was
I kept my composure.
Hands in pockets,
legs locked,
muscles so tense in the cold air that they ached from the shock
turned to anger that rippled apart
inside me.

Two years later my best friend at that school would fall in love
with him.

Time went on how it did until one day after school,
he and she,
intertwined the way lovers are,
he pulled away to talk about his ways and without hesitation,
I called him a redneck.

Moments later catching up to me as I sat behind the wheel of
my gold `97 Altima he leaned into my
driver window, eye to eye with me he opened his mouth to say,
"If I'm a redneck, then you're a
nigger."—But no noise went unheard,
no muscle in my body froze.
A rage exploded inside me that beat against my chest and
climbed up out of my throat.

"Don't you ever in your fucking life call me that again."

THAT SOUTHERN THING

I stared into his penetrating eyes once more before tearing off,
leaving the parking lot. Speeding
down the road, that familiar ache in my stomach came back
once more as warm salty tears formed
around the brim of my eyes spilling down my cheeks.

I'd eventually go off to university, leaving almost everything
from high school behind.

The summer after graduating, Zimmerman was acquitted.
Trayvon was no less murdered.

I learned to be angry and that it was okay to be angry.

I'd go off to school to learn words like white supremacy and
anti-blackness
and how to voice the concepts of things I always knew yet
never knew how to articulate. I'd go on to
attend protests in North Carolina.

Blue lights flickered against the backdrop
of a December night in `14,
a deafening ringing in my ears,
Durham riot police moved toward the crowd,
throwing protestors to the ground.
Tears spilled down my cheeks as I angrily looked a black
officer in his eyes.
We didn't change anything that night, but we were angry.

I'd begin to attend spoken words.
Standing on a stage
with the shaky legs of an amateur,
the glow of a phone screen on my face
while I read a poem I wrote on the beauty of black women.

My hands trembled yet I learned to find my voice in spaces
All That I Could Say

where they weren't welcome.

Despite all of that, at twenty-two, I saw that old classmate one
night leaving a sweaty bar, the music
deafening, and in spite of the alcohol coursing through my
blood, the sobering feeling of the past
jolted through my body. His heavy stare laid upon me with a
smirk on his face and like at fifteen
I froze.

"You married now?" he eventually inquired.
He dehumanized you, don't answer him.
"No."
"Have any kids now?"
Spit in his face. He doesn't need to know anything about you.

"No," a voice responded.

As I walked away,
my clothes clung to my clammy skin.
The breath finally
expelled from my lungs.
I walked away that night feeling defeated—but not by him.
The voice I had learned to find
somehow abandoned me that night.

I said all that I could say ... yet I didn't say enough. •

Copyright 2020, Lauren Summers

Lauren Summers is a writer and poet from Greensboro, NC, who is
a graduate from UNCG with a B.A. in English and minor in
German. While she enjoys writing speculative fiction, her poetry
often deals with themes of love, loss, self-reflection, and hope.
She plans to pursue her MFA and thereafter publish.

Our "Wild"-life Sanctuary
by Charles Davenport, Jr.

We called my younger brother "Snake Eyes," not because of some hideous birth defect, but because he was always the first to see serpents, which we encountered often. His was not the only nickname: mine was "Bubba," and our two best friends were "Flea" and "Turtle."

In the mid-70s, our neighborhood in Greensboro, North Carolina, was surrounded by woods, lakes, and streams—what today would be called "greenspace." Nearby was Jefferson Country Club, the centerpiece of a massive wildlife sanctuary.

On that glorious expanse of field and forest we camped, played football, tossed frisbees, and even rode motorcycles. Technically, if you're a stickler for rules, you could say we were trespassing on private property. And we knew it, because we were routinely pursued by the club's elite golf cart-driving security force.

But they never caught us. Very few vehicles can match the blistering speed of adolescent males fleeing the scene of an offense. Golf carts certainly can't. Besides, we were intimately familiar with the trails in those woods, so the security detail was easy to elude. Typically, as soon as we fled—laughing and stumbling into the nearest thicket—"Barney Fife" would peel off and head back to the clubhouse. I suspect Jefferson's officials didn't take our trespassing too seriously. We didn't either.

In fact, for several consecutive summers, we created a "swimming hole" by damming the stream that ran through the property. From those muddy banks, over and over again we launched ourselves, barefoot, in cut-off blue jeans.

We refined our cannonball technique as if we were preparing for the Olympics. The performance of each "diver" was critiqued and rated by his colleagues. In retrospect, those critiques also served an educational purpose: we all became proficient in the art of profane oratory. Our schoolteachers' lesson plans in that realm were woefully inadequate.

But let us return to the solemn matter at hand: When evaluating a cannonball, the diver's technique—often highly unorthodox—was less important than the critical, make-or-break "splash rating."

The quality of a belly-flop, we learned, was most accurately assessed five minutes or so after the performance, by which time, if the diver's form were exemplary, his face and stomach would have turned a glowing, purplish-red. Bonus points were awarded for a resounding splat! upon the artist's contact with the water, and also if he had trouble breathing upon emerging from the water. The truly majestic belly-flop encompassed all three elements: a deafening splat! that foretold respiratory difficulty and blistered skin.

Young boys go about their business with reckless abandon, oblivious to potential peril. This was particularly true of "Flea" and "Turtle"; they feared nothing. In hindsight, I realize hazards could have been lurking in our swimming hole—large rocks or stumps, for instance, concealed under the surface of the murky water.

But we were keenly aware of only one danger—snakes. With alarming frequency, our half-mile walk from the neighborhood to the swimming hole was highlighted by serpent encounters— sometimes two or three in a single outing.

It was disconcerting when we were strolling casually through a dense forest to have a fellow hiker point and shriek, "Snake!" But only those timely (albeit hysteria-inducing) warnings from "Snake Eyes" prevented us from stepping on and being "lit-up" by a sunbathing black snake, or a copperhead, or worse, the dreaded and feared water moccasin.

An age-old bit of Southern folklore recounts swimmers or divers (the tale has several versions) blundering into a "nest" of water moccasins. According to the legend, several frolicking, unsuspecting water-sports enthusiasts have been killed in such a fashion, felled by multiple venom-injecting bites. One afternoon, after our return home from the swimming hole, Dad shared one version of the story with "Snake Eyes" and me. We never went back to the creek.

Our "Wild"-life Sanctuary

Decades later, I learned that the spine-tingling stories about nesting water moccasins were completely false. I'm pretty sure Dad knew that. But he also had a healthy sense of humor, and he wasn't going to let mere facts get in the way of inflicting years' worth of good-natured terror on his sons.

Decades ago, that wildlife sanctuary was bulldozed to make way for apartments, schools, restaurants, and shopping centers. A grocery store sits where my childhood home once stood. The lake and the creek are gone. The fields and forests—our football fields and motorcycle trails—exist only in nostalgic memory.

To some folks, development engenders a sense of progress. I disagree. The words describing such "progress" drift into my head as time-traveling fugitives from the artful, profane oratory we mastered while belly-flopping into our swimming hole deep in those forbidden woods where "Bubba," "Flea," "Turtle," and "Snake Eyes" used to play. •

Charles Davenport Jr. (cdavenportjr@hotmail.com) has been an op-ed columnist at the *News & Record* (Greensboro, North Carolina) for 15 years. His debut novel, *The Closure Committee*, was published in 2018, and he is working on a sequel. His favorite scribbler is George Gissing, an English novelist of the Victorian era. Charles and his wife live in Kernersville, North Carolina, with their three spoiled "kids": a giddy Golden Retriever and two haughty felines.

Biscuit Weaver

by Gary Neil Gupton

A unt Nobia didn't have any children, but she mothered several, all the same. Neither a homemaker, she nevertheless knew how to make extraordinary biscuits. I had just seen her Christmas Eve, but I wanted to stop by her house on my way back to Wake Forest University from my parent's Franklin County homeplace.

The school used to be a Baptist seminary before it moved to Winston-Salem in 1956, so, dancing was banned on campus until 1957. A decade later, the college became a university, and Northerners invaded. A dozen years on, this Southern boy joined them.

Aunt Nobia's little, green, asbestos-sided house was set back less than ten yards off NC Highway 56, just outside of Louisburg before you get to Pruitt Lumber Company. I turned onto the gravel driveway that circled her house. The recapped tires on my '65 Mustang were so close to the edge of her pond that I could hang my head out the window and look down into the green, slimy water.

Cane poles hung out in the shed, their tips pointing toward the water waiting for children to take them fishing. Fishing worms wriggled at the end of the drain line that ran from Aunt Nobia's washing machine.

Aunt Nobia used to ride show horses when she was younger, sporting a riding cap, britches, and black leather boots. Years later when she couldn't ride anymore, she helped Uncle Jack make and break donkeys and horses into little mules. "Break" was not really a good word for what she did; she "made" them. (I didn't know until years later how they made mules out of their donkeys and horses. It's an intimate process.)

When we wanted to go fishing—and not dig worms—Aunt Nobia made our bait. She'd whip up a batch of biscuit dough from scratch or open a can of Pillsbury from the fridge. Raw dough wouldn't stay on the hook unless she weaved in cotton from balls usually reserved for smearing pink calamine lotion on poison ivy rash.

For quick bait, she smacked the biscuit can on the edge of the speckled green countertop. Pop! We'd jump. A white blob bulged out the side of the spiraled cardboard.

Tippy toed we'd stand by Aunt Nobia's ample hips, eager to get our hands in the dough. She would let us mash the discs of white dough, flecked with slivers of shortening hard as candlewax, with the heels of our pink, tender hands while she pinched and pulled the rubbery edges of the dough. She would pluck a cotton ball from the medicine cabinet and pull at the white fibers like she was preparing it for a spinning jenny.

When the fluffy ball was spider-webby and flat, she'd spread it over the flattened dough.

We children stepped back, wary of Aunt Nobia's elbows as she kneaded and weaved the cotton into a mini loaf. But she wasn't going to bake it. She rolled marbles of cotton-reinforced dough, one by one, for our fish bait. She swatted our behinds and shooed us out the storm door. "You better catch some!" She knew we would catch little bass, easy and plentiful from her overstocked pond.

That was a long time ago. I looked up at the storm door, halfway expecting to hear Ringo, her white, English bulldog, stampeding down the hall. Ringo had died years ago; Aunt Nobia stilled missed him.

"Come on in!" Aunt Nobia greeted me with a big, buxom hug. I sat down at the breakfast nook, reminded of a booth at the Boulevard Drive-in.

"Want me to make you some biscuits? No trouble." She smiled and opened the sturdy white Frigidaire, fumbling around for buttermilk. She stood up with a viable substitute, a quart jar of Duke's mayonnaise in hand. "If all else fails ..."

Out of the cabinet she took down her yellow, melamine bowl, hollowed out a mound of Red Band self-rising flour and plopped a four-finger blob of mayonnaise on the heap, exploding flour dust into the air. She pinched off a bit of dough, rolled it into a marble and offered it from the palm of her hand.

Biscuit Weaver

"No cotton," she said with a wink.

I popped the doughball into my mouth and rolled it around on my tongue, savoring it. In a few minutes Aunt Nobia pulled the black metal pan from the oven. Warm golden brown, crusty-topped biscuits invited me to stay.

"I've got to go, Aunt Nobia."
"Already?"

She wrapped the biscuits in parchment then crinkled shiny aluminum foil around to keep them warm.

She gave me her homemade biscuits, another warm hug, and a welcomed peck on the cheek. As I drove past the pond and looked back, I could see Aunt Nobia—and a dear childhood memory—waving goodbye. •

Copyright 2020, Gary Neil Gupton

Gary Neil Gupton lives in Leland, North Carolina, where he is a member of the NC Writers Network, the Latino Book Club and is editor of the Magnolia Greens community newsletter. He published a children's chap book, *Time to Meet Max*, set in Guatemala. Many of his stories are set in other countries, but they always seem to come back to his roots in North Carolina where he grew up on a small farm.

Southern Exposure
by Ron Machado

My first "southern exposure" came in late winter while I was traveling from West Texas to South Carolina. I had just finished training as an Air Force pilot and was going to be stationed in Sumter, South Carolina. To me, even that name sounded backwoods and "hick-ish."

After driving through the world's worse ice storm in Atlanta, I pulled into South Carolina after midnight. My sports car was coated in ice! I was staying at a friend's place for a couple of days before going down to Florida for some intermediate training. He was finishing his training, and the plan was for me to take over his apartment lease.

The next day my friend, Paul, introduced me to his neighbor Michael. Michael was a little shorter than me, a little rounder, and had a beard. Then he spoke. I could tell he had an accent, but other than that I had no earthly idea what he said. Then he leaned over to one side and spit on the sidewalk. Upon closer examination I noticed one of Michael's cheeks bulged out more than the other. I shook his hand and told him I was glad to meet him, and then Paul and I left to ride to the base to sign in with my new unit and check out the area. I told my friend I had no idea what Michael had said. Paul just laughed and said, "You'll get used to it."

Soon I was on my way to Florida for the additional training course. It was a long drive and about half way through, somewhere in Georgia, I stopped for dinner. I don't remember the name of the restaurant, but the food smelled good and the décor was clean and homey looking.

I was seated by the hostess and began looking at the menu. I was 23 years old at the time and single. When the waitress came up to my table, she introduced herself. My recollection was she was middle aged like my mother. She started off by saying, "What can I get you to drink, Sugar?" During subsequent stops at my table to take my order and refill my drink, she called me "Honey," "Sweetie," and "Sugar" again. I was very uncomfortable. I had never been hit on before, especially by an older woman! Needless to say, it was a very quick meal and I was back on the road as fast I could get there.

After a year or so of living in South Carolina, I did begin to understand my neighbor Michael, and I even got used to his spitting tobacco juice in the middle of sentences. One day, a knock at my door revealed Michael standing there with a plate of food.

"Here, try some of this," he said. It was a large, generous portion, and it smelled really good. I asked him what it was.

"Venison stew."

I had never eaten venison before, or any other wild game animal. I don't think I was opposed to it, but in Southern California folks don't do much deer hunting. I thanked Michael, took the plate in, and sat down to eat. I wasn't sure what to expect, but it was delicious! It was the first of several plates of venison stew Michael brought over.

Eventually, I met a girl through church. She was very nice and said things like, "I declare," "Y'all," and "Bless your heart." One day she invited me to dinner with her family. We had fried chicken, homemade rolls, home-grown green beans, and mashed potatoes—made from real potatoes! The smell of those rolls and fried chicken caused my stomach to growl as soon as I walked in. It was the best meal I ever had. She called her dad "Sir," and her mom "Ma'am." Her dad called her mom "Sugar."

Well, a little while later I married that Southern girl and we have four Southern daughters who say "Y'all," Bless your heart," and they call their dad "Sir" and their mom "Ma'am." We spent several years moving around this country and others during my time in the Air Force, but when it was time to end my career and decide where we were going to live, it was an easy choice. We came back to South Carolina.

As a lot of other people have said before me, "I wasn't born here, but I got here as quick as I could." •

Southern Exposure

Kenneth R Machado (Ron) lives in Rock Hill, South Carolina where he works for a large international energy company. He spent 13 years previously as an Air Force pilot. This is his first published work. With his Air Force background and four incredibly talented daughters, he feels he will have enough material to write more than a few good stories. He is currently working on a manuscript that he hopes to submit for publishing later this year.

Erline's Kitchen

by Bill Gramley

I moved from Pennsylvania to Winston-Salem, North Carolina, in 1949 when I was 13. I noted cases of Tru-Ade and Dr. Pepper on the porch, found out what pinto beans were and collard greens, grits, and then pimento cheese. It took a while, but I learned to like these new foods and the sodas. But that was only an introduction to what I would find on a small family farm in Rowan County.

Just before my senior year at Davidson College, I went on a blind date to Montreat College and met Kathy Steele. I soon enough found out we were born on the same day (a mere 500 miles apart), and we began our courtship. We married two years later. Her family lived on unpaved Baker Mill Road in a well-weathered wooden house heated with firewood. They had an outhouse (which was new to me, a city boy). As time went by, I observed life on the farm and even helped scrape the hair off the scalded carcasses at hog-killing time in several Novembers.

Her mother was Erline, and she ran the kitchen. When I was there for breakfast, I remember either orange juice or homemade tomato juice and hot coffee with real cream on the table. There were toasted slices of her own yeast bread, a jar of preserved pink grape jelly, and butter that she had processed and poured into an attractive round wooden mold and set out upon a green, glass-covered plate. This was butter distinctively flavored from the grasses where the cows pastured. These were but side dishes to the main course of hot, white corn meal mush (finer-ground than grits) accompanied with thin, dark brown gravy, and eggs from the coop around back, scrambled and a little runny; and slices of fried ham, cured with red and black pepper rubbed in and aged by hanging in burlap sacks out in a shed.

In the summertime there would also be slices of cantaloupe at hand, already peeled for my fork to spear. She had none of the modern-day fast-food coffee-and-biscuit stuff. This was a meal worth getting up for, say some time around seven just after Kathy's father, William, had already milked the cows and his appetite was ready for some serious business.

William had come in and removed his boots and pith helmet, huffing and wheezing a bit after washing the milking equipment. He had on bib overalls under his blue jean jacket. He might growl something or cough a bit as he took his place at one end of the table and offered grace. If William wanted something not within easy reach, he would usually ask for it in a round-about fashion: "I believe I'll have some of that bread now." Later he would take a little cloth bag of tobacco out of his upper bib pocket and roll his own cigarette, lick the paper, and light it from a wooden match struck against a rough surface, usually the underside of the table. I had never seen anything like that before and was intrigued by the process.

The radio had been on softly prior to the meal as it would be later in the morning as Erline listened regularly to the music and news and began to prepare what would be the main meal of the day at noon, as though breakfast was but a foretaste of glory divine yet to come.

When I got up from the breakfast table, feeling content and ready for the day ahead, I noticed the African violets on tables and windowsills, dabs of pink and purple amidst their fuzzy green leaves. Erline obviously knew something about gardening, for they were always healthy or on their way to becoming so. They were a sure sign of the touches of beauty this farming woman added to life, to her home, and to those who had eyes to see.

This Southern family farm was never much of a money-maker, but the milk and the hogs, the wool from the sheep, a bit of cotton in earlier years, and grain and corn for the animals were the basics. She saw to it, when years were lean, that her four children were well fed, even if it was cornbread and molasses. It was always enough.

Sometimes Erline served persimmon pudding and she always made a fresh coconut cake with real whipped cream for our birthdays, hers being the same day as ours. And in good times and rough, she might invite the minister's family from the Presbyterian Church down the road for Sunday dinner. That's Southern hospitality at its best and I hope it doesn't fade away. Certainly, my memories of it and of Erline's kitchen have not.•

Erline's Kitchen

Bill Gramley is a retired Moravian minister. In recent years he has written several "Devotional Expressions and Prayers" booklets through Centenary United Methodist Church in Winston-Salem. He writes in the Senior Games Literary Arts category each year and stays active competing in track and field, mostly as a shot put, discus, and hammer thrower, winning the Masters national discus championship in 2019 for men aged 80-84. He and his wife, Sandra, live in Lewisville, North Carolina.

.

Country Love and Marriage
by Joe Brown

I read just the other day that the average cost for a wedding in North Carolina is around $25,000!

Mercy sakes alive, mine cost only $5 and not just because I'm cheap!

In my sophomore year of high school, I saw this girl, Margaret Faye Anderson, who had just joined our class. I asked around and found out that her dad had kept her home from school to help in the tobacco crop. Being a good hand at working in the tobacco fields, I decided to introduce myself. Right off I had this feeling that she was the one for me!

By the end of that year I had presented her with a going-steady ring, and on Christmas Eve of 1969, I gave her an engagement ring. I purchased it at Brindle's in Elkin, and although not huge it was perfect for a lifetime of marriage for a country couple.

Fast-forward to graduation and all the preparations had been made. We had rented a small 450 sqft cabin/house next door to my sister's house in Hamptonville. It came mostly furnished and we added the hope chest filled, as it was, with all the dishes—the Gulf station gave a set with each fill-up—sheets, towels, etc. we had been collecting.

We had been to the courthouse and got the necessary forms and licensees. When there I had inquired of the Clerk about when we could get married. She told us that after going to the hospital for blood testing we would be all set and could get married whenever we wanted. So, after getting the blood test, we thought we were all ready.

My mother had contributed the making of a beautifully simple wedding dress for the big day, and a neighbor friend agreed to fix Margaret's hair into a bun that was popular in those days.

We were all ready for the big week. On Tuesday, June 2, 1970, we graduated from high school. On June 5th, Margaret's Mom and close neighbor made up the Bride's party, my Mom and Dad made up mine. We all met on the courthouse square at 10 a.m., and since I had arranged and called that meeting, I asked everyone to wait there while I ran in and made sure all was a "GO." Boy, did the Clerk burst my bubble! She informed me that the judge was in session and would not be available until the end of the day. Wow! That did not fit into my plans at all.

"Is there anyone else in town who could do the ceremony?" I asked."

"Ed across the street is a Justice of the Peace. Maybe he would be willing to do It."

That was her only suggestion. Well, I hightailed it out the door, and as I was coming down the courthouse steps, looked over at the "wedding party." They looked very confused as I held up my hand and hollered, "Wait there. I'll be right back."

Imagine this: an 18-year-old boy running across Main Street in Mocksville, trying to find someone to say the words that would change him into a man. Well, Ed was there and when I asked if he could marry us, he asked "When?" I responded "Right now!"

He agreed that he could and declared that he would, so I fetched the waiting folks and we all squeezed into the very small office of Ed's TV Repair Shop. I showed him our legal documents and Ed commenced to asking us if we would. We did, and so it was all over in a few minutes. Ed showed us where to sign; he did likewise. I paid Ed $5 for his services, resulting in Margaret and I being just as married as anyone else in the whole world.

Our reception was on the sidewalk, where we said goodbye to the family and headed our `56 Chevy into the mountains. We spent our honeymoon at a small hotel in Transylvania County. My new Job started on Monday the 8th, and since funds were very limited, we were back to our little house on Saturday night.

On January 20, 1990, Margaret died. The doctors said it was a

Country Love and Marriage

71

very unusual type of brain cancer. She had migraines and was seeing doctors, but one day she was raking leaves in the yard and the next day she was gone.

So, for young and old alike thinking of marriage, it's not the venue, gown, caterer, photographer, shower, gifts, cake, music, rehearsal dinner, the Bahama honeymoon, etc. No, sir! It's the love that's in your hearts, the perseverance, and the dedication to each other that makes a successful marriage.

And a $5 justice of the peace will do just fine. •

Joseph Brown is a native of North Carolina, born in Yadkin County and reared in Davie County. He now resides in the Bethania area of Forsyth County and has lived all his life within 40 miles of his birthplace. In February 2020 he retired from 50 years in the construction industry. Most of his previous writing has been daily journals on his mission trips to Kentucky, Canada, and Ecuador. His first published story was in 2019 Personal Essay Publishing Project, *Exploring*..

.

Not Finished Yet

by Suzanne Cottrell

When I first moved to Wilson, North Carolina, from Trumansburg, New York, in 1974, my blended Midwestern and Northern ears agonized over the slow speech of the residents. I retrieved their words like reeling in fish. However, in my haste, I lost some fish, misunderstood words, and annoyed my conversational partners when my tongue and teeth formed words to finish their sentences.

With my jaw clenched and my head tilted toward Alan, a new teaching colleague. *Did he say he was from "Garner" or "Ghana?" Are we in North Carolina or Africa?* I cringed with each dropped "r" and ending "g." I pressed my hands to my ears. *Please enunciate.* Emphasizing the "r," I asked, "Alan, did you say Garner?"

"Yes," he said.

Deciphering his speech was like learning a foreign language. I recalled the challenge of accent placement in Spanish; yet, it didn't make a difference with some words in English. For example, I grew up saying pa-KäN, but most North Carolinians say PEE-kan. No matter how one pronounced the word, my mouth watered with the smells of maple and roasted nuts of a pecan pie. Nevertheless, my ears preferred the refined sound of pa-KäN.

I used to say, "You guys, please turn off the lights." Now I say, "Y'all, please cut off the lights." I don't recall when this idiomatic transformation occurred. My husband told me he said "cut off the lights" because many American colonists cut off a candle's wick instead of snuffing out the flame. That made sense. For several months, I practiced blending "you" and "all." At last, a smoothed "y'all" flowed out of my mouth as a one syllable contraction. I was proud of this accomplishment; however, my northern relatives and friends laughed and mocked my "y'all." But I just played along.

"Are you trying to sound like a Southerner?"

"Well, I'm married to a Southern, and my family and I live in North Carolina," I explained.

My snail-paced assimilation switched to softening my hard vowel sounds. On one trip to visit my dad and stepmom on Grand Island, New York, my husband and I puzzled over my stepmom's pronunciation of a destination on their itinerary for us. After lunch, she said, "We're taking you to a special exhibit at ät päk."

My husband and I raised our brows and looked at each other. "Do you know where we're going?" My husband asked me.

"No, I didn't understand her," I said. "Katie, where are we going?"
She repeated, "ät päk."

I hunched my shoulders and lifted my hands, palms up. "Katie, how do you spell that?"

"A-R-T-P-A-R-K," she enunciated.

"Oh, Art Park." I winked at my husband.

Several years later, my husband, daughter, and I visited friends in Albany, New York, on our way to Connecticut. While we waited for our food at an IHOP, I heard the rapid, clipped speech of the other customers like horse hooves clicking on pavement. Their "a's" sounded like "awe's."

I turned to my husband and said, "They talk funny."

My daughter covered her mouth and giggled. My husband laughed, too.

"What's so funny?" I asked.

"You used to talk like that," my husband said.

"Did I really sound like that?"

My daughter smiled knowingly, and my husband nodded his head. "Yep."

I've lived in North Carolina 45 years and have become accustomed to the North Carolina dialect and lifestyle. I now much prefer both. I speak more slowly with drawn-out long vowel sounds, yet I'll probably never sound like a true Southerner. I still have a trace of my Midwestern nasality, a hint of my Buckeye birthplace.

I have not yet mastered the nuances of "bless your heart," nor have I acquired a taste for sweet tea. A few weeks ago, a friend and I had lunch at a diner near Clayton, North Carolina. I ordered a glass of "iced tea." With my first sip, I puckered

Not Finished Yet

my lips and opened my eyes wide. "My, that is really sweet!"

"We drink our tea sweet, dear," our waitress declared, then added almost under her breath, "Bless your heart."

Her tone stung like I should have known that tea in the South was always sweet. *Wasn't that, of course, what sugar, honey, or artificial sweeteners were for?* I just smiled and asked for a glass of water. My taste buds regret each time I forget to specify "unsweetened."

One of my husband's aunts frequently says, "Bless your heart" as she smiles and pats your hand. I hadn't imagined the meaning of a single expression could be so difficult to understand. I am still learning to interpret people's tones, inflections, volume, and facial expressions to get the real meaning of what they are saying. My transformation is not finished yet.

Bless my heart. •

Suzanne Cottrell, a member of the Granville County Writers' Group and NC Writers' Network, lives with her husband and three rescue dogs in rural Granville County, North Carolina. An outdoor enthusiast and retired teacher, she enjoys reading, writing, knitting, hiking, Pilates, and Tai Chi. Her prose has appeared in numerous journals and anthologies, including *Bearing Up*, *Exploring*, *Pop Machine*, *Unwanted Visitors*, *Empty Silos*, *Dragon Poet Review*, *Dual Coast Magazine*, *Parks and Points*, and *Nailpolish Stories, A Tiny and Colorful Literary Journal*.

Casket Shopping
by Karen Luke Jackson

"The thought of a casket closing over my face sends shivers down my spine," Mama said whenever the conversation turned to funerals. "I can't breathe. It's like I'm being smothered."

Mama's trepidation about being trapped in a coffin increased as she entered her eighties and as she began to diminish. Planning her funeral bloomed into an obsession. She eventually convinced Daddy, my younger sister Janis, and me that she'd get some peace of mind if she could pick out the casket in which she'd be buried.

After college, I'd married and moved from Ocilla, Georgia, to North Carolina. Janis and her husband, Oscar, had returned to our hometown and lived across the street from our parents.

"Daddy wants *me* to take Mama casket shopping,"
Janis announced during a phone visit.
"We'll do it together," I assured her, "on my next trip down."

That fall, Mama rode shotgun and Janis slung jokes from the back as I drove to Paulk Funeral Home. When I parked beside the ramp to the mortuary's entrance, my sister hopped out and opened Mama's door. Swinging her legs from the Buick's front seat, Mama reached for Janis' arm and pulled herself erect.

"Let me get the walker out of the trunk," I called as I hurried to the rear of the car. For the last year, that contraption had been Mama's constant companion at the house and on frequent doctors' visits.

"No!" Mama declared, taking her first step toward the building. "I'm walking into that place on my own steam. Give me your arm, Karen."

Flanking her sides, Janis and I supported most of Mama's weight. She skittered more quickly than we ever thought possible down the sidewalk, up the ramp, and into the parlor where the funeral director, dressed in his standard black suit and horn-rimmed glasses, met us.

"It's so good to see you, Miss Eloise," Rick said, giving Mama a gentle hug then greeting us with a smile. He knew our parents well. Despite Mama's fear, they had dueted at many a funeral in Irwin County.

"Where's Mr. O. L.? Parking the car?"
"No, he had other business," Mama replied. "But I'm here to pick out my casket."

Daddy did *not* have other business. He had declined the outing because three women selecting a burial box were, for him, two too many. However, before we left the house, he'd told Janis and me to buy whatever would comfort her.

Rick pointed us toward an elevator. We rode to the second floor where the merchandise was on display. After perusing the room, Mama gravitated toward a white French Provincial with a newborn-pink lining. Janis and I stood beside her to offer support.

"I'd feel like I was sleeping if I were laid out in this one," she said fingering the silky fabric, "but I'm not so sure about the color. I like the white smocked lining in the bronze coffin on the other side better."

Rick, who'd been standing a respectable distance away, heard Mama's comment.

"The French Provincial only comes with the pink lining," he said, "unless I put in a special order. That would take several weeks."
"Well, we've got time," Janis said.
"Can you store the casket until she needs it?" I asked.
"Sure can."

My sister and I shot each other knowing glances. "She'll take it," we said, almost in unison.

Rick didn't ask Mama to sign any papers; said he'd bill Daddy. Nor did he treat us to coffee and cake, like the funeral director did Clyde Edgerton's sisters in *Walking Across Egypt*. To satisfy our hunger and to celebrate, we took Mama to The Shoppes for lunch. There she ambulated with her walker from car to café. Once seated, she feasted on her usual chicken salad sandwich and iced tea.

That evening, Janis and I sat with Daddy around the butcher

Casket Shopping

block in the kitchen and described the casket Mama had selected. We were preparing him for what it cost when she walked into the room, poured herself a cup of decaf coffee, and joined us at the table.

"The girls told me you found something you liked," Daddy said, still clueless about the price tag.
"I did," she grinned, "and what's more, I've got an announcement to make."

Mama placed the cup she'd been cradling on a red placemat and cleared her throat. "O. L., we have the most wonderful daughters in the world, and today was the most fun I've had in a long time. In fact, it was one of the best days of my life."

Janis and I beamed. And later that night, when Daddy learned how much that special-order casket was going to set him back, he crowed, "Girls, it was worth every penny." •

Oral history, contemplative practices, and clowning inspire Karen Luke Jackson's stories and poems, which have appeared in numerous journals, including *Ruminate*, *Great Smokies Review*, *Kakalak*, *ONE*, *Emrys Journal*, *Friends Journal* and *moonShine review*. A facilitator with the Center for Courage & Renewal, Karen resides in a cottage on a goat pasture in Flat Rock, North Carolina. There she writes and companions people on their spiritual journeys. *GRIT*, a chapbook chronicling her sister's life as Clancey the Clown, is forthcoming in 2020. For more, visit www.karenlukejackson.com.

Spouse in the House
by R. Lee Riley

I t's not as if we didn't know what we were getting
ourselves into when moving south in 2005. We were a
brave, young couple escaping the stuffy, cold, gray recesses
of Ivy League urban worldliness, suddenly plunging ourselves
into unknown rural, green overgrowth and vast open Carolina
blue sky. We were idealism incarnate not yet tasting Sweet Tea.

Seven years in new sun quickly passed, and though we had
found fond new clans next door adequately distanced from our
doorstep, we began to sense great disturbances in wider local
perception of our white picket fence. In spring of 2012
Southern hospitality suddenly went as sour as a Yankee
learning what "Bless Your Heart" really means.

"Amendment One" in North Carolina was putting democracy
in action by asking a small sliver of voters on Primary Day if
some of its citizens should be forever barred from the same
rights everyone else has to obtain a license to marry, or
become certified as a couple officially. Yes, a Constitutional
clarification vote was needed to deny a state permit to fellow
citizens guilty of no crimes, who contributed to society and

shared lives like everyone else with a brick ranch home and a John Deere ride-on mower, yet whom some groups somehow pitchfork-despised as degenerates unworthy of legitimacy under law.

I've been to a lot of places as a kid in an uncomfortable suit. Weddings, funerals, you know – formal affairs. And growing up educated in school by faded Highlights cartoons showing me and young Billy how America was founded on freedom and the rights for all, well, even as a kid something always struck me as odd and made me feel all itchy and uncomfortable when it was spoken aloud at church weddings.

> "By the power vested in me by the great State of Rhode Island and Providence Plantations, I now pronounce you husband and wife."

Makes you sit upright in a walnut pew, doesn't it? New England is appropriate for this conversation. A cold place where Puritans escaped to practice their faith, but whose banished upstarts led to the great Providence of me. While I enjoy the symbolism of my ancestral trajectory in matters of the Spirit, consider the young and too-tight-tied me sitting there, amid hymnal references and saint-stained windows, baffled at how a priest could suddenly be the mayor at a ribbon cutting ceremony. That childhood memory inspired me at an Uptown Charlotte public forum. When it was my turn to speak, I bared my new tar-heeled Yankee hybrid heart to my supposedly Southern hospitable friends assembled there in the round:

"Problem is, we all gave the priest the power in the first place. The issue is not how to define marriage, the issue before us is whether or not we want to destroy Democracy. Now the Church, in whatever cloth it chooses today, wants to actually legislate its banned behavior doctrine by scribbling on the state Constitution that gives you the very right not to listen to a single thing that church says.

I'm sorry if that's a bad old bee in your big-bowed Easter Bonnet, and I frankly don't care to hear about your Bible babble or the inability of two rockets to make offspring. To be in favor of an Amendment to existing law already banning same-gender matrimony is overkill. Such overkill is based in hate, and not at all in practicing principles of universal love found in any Savior's heart.

There are two marriages on the table, and nobody is seeing it—the one the Church performs as sacrament and the one the State sees as a stamp of approval by some Justice of the Peace. This approving stamp, however, does not require the former but can in fact be performed by the State. We only want the one the State sees, thank you, and we'll find a pretty little chapel later.

For over two decades I have loved and shared my life with my partner, companion, significant other—any euphemism you so choose, but whose role in my life is most definitely spouse. Our home is lovely, we invest in society jointly. Our family recognizes us as such. So do

Spouse in the House

83

our friends and neighbors. For this, I want to check
one little box, called spouse."

Well, we lost. On TV, a petty lady in a white church jacket and
hat from a family-values group mockingly sliced a wedding
cake at a victory party. We waited, second class, three years,
until in the summer of 2015 when as if by some Union re-
enactment in reconstruction of Democracy, came rights-denied
bestowed once again. Nowadays, I do enjoy sweet Southern
Sundays. I have a husband stamped downtown, and friends
from afar share my porch like birds in a Disney cartoon. •

R. Lee Riley earned his B.A. in Journalism and in early life recorded
news, audio novels, and poetry for the national non-profit Radio
Reading Services. Today he lives in Salisbury, North Carolina and is a
member of Winston Salem Writers. His writing is included in *Flying
South*'s 2016 anthology, and he's been featured on posters for Poetry
in Plain Sight several years running. Lee has also been awarded Silver
and Bronze medals for his winning poetry selections in Rowan
County's 2018 and 2019 Silver Arts Festival.

That Ain't the Way My Daddy Do It!
by Joel R. Stegall

When I was in elementary school in the early Fifties, my father's work as a Baptist pastor required our family to move from Winston-Salem, North Carolina, to a tiny village in the eastern part of the state. The economy there was based almost entirely on tobacco farming.

In this community, education was not a high priority. North Carolina law required students to stay in school until age 16, but quite a few of my new classmates assumed they would drop out as soon as they reached that magical birthday. After all, you didn't need to know how to solve quadratic equations or diagram a sentence to guide a plow behind a mule or pull leaves off a tobacco stalk.

I thought my new elementary school was almost primitive. Control of student behavior, apparently the primary educational objective, was largely through intimidation and fear of bodily harm. One teacher, Mrs. Redfern (a pseudonym), had a reputation for throwing books and erasers at those who did not respond submissively to verbal threats. If flying objects didn't work, she could always bring out her paddle. Even this radical approach was not guaranteed to bring the result intended. The year before we arrived, I was told, after Mrs. Redfern had paddled a particularly obstreperous boy, the boy's mama showed up at school and "whupped Mrs. Redfern's ass."

But most days, school was just unrelentingly boring. Not only were the classes dreary, there were no athletic teams, no physical education classes, no music ensembles, no drama groups, no clubs. It didn't take long for me to dread school. I began to understand why students quit as soon as they could.

Even recess was a mixed respite. Kids were turned loose on the playground while the teachers went to the lounge to smoke. Some of us boys played basketball on the hard dirt of the parking lot where a backboard and bare hoop had been bolted atop a shaky wood pole. With testosterone beginning to infiltrate our 13- and 14-year-old bodies, and with no adult supervision, disagreements frequently became physical altercations. Usually these were of no consequence, but once in a while a fight would break out and some tattler would run to the teachers' lounge to find a teacher, who would have to put out her cigarette, trudge out to the school yard, and haul the ne'er-do-wells in for a scolding.

I tried to avoid fights, not so much on account of Jesus' teaching about turning the other cheek as because I was one of the smaller boys and didn't want to get, in the vernacular, "my ass whupped." But one day a particularly obnoxious little redneck, Jimmy James (another pseudonym), finding he couldn't defend against my emerging ball-handling skills, jumped on my back.

Jimmy was no bigger than I, and I threw him off. He got up and hit me. We exchanged punches. I thought I was getting the better of it when a teacher pulled us apart for the mandatory reprimand. But it was worth it. Word got around that I was not to be messed with.

LESSON #1: Jesus may have been right with that thing about the other cheek but defending myself sure felt good.

Despite oppressive classrooms, hilarious moments sometimes erupted unexpectedly. Our social studies class included a unit on alcohol, presumably intended as a warning about the evils of strong drink. Inexplicably, the textbook included instructions for distilling spirits. In a place and time when illegal moonshine provided significant supplemental income for a lot of farmers, did someone really think farm boys needed help with how to make hooch?

In class, our teacher, Mrs. Redfern—famous for hurling things at students—tried to explain the distillation process outlined in the book. Jimmy James, the boy I had fought with, became visibly agitated, shaking his head and frantically waving his hand. When Mrs. Redfern finally recognized him, Jimmy proclaimed with the certainty of a revival preacher, "That ain't the way my daddy do it." He then launched into a rather impressive lecture on how moonshine was supposed to be made.

LESSON #2: We often reject new ideas simply because they are different from what we have previously learned from someone we trust.

That Ain't the Way My Daddy Do It!

To this day, when I find myself debunking an opinion that differs from my own, somewhere in the back of my mind I hear, "That ain't the way my daddy do it." Once in a while this awareness allows me to step back and ask if a different way of looking at things and doing things might be valid. I suspect Mrs. Redfern could have been better served by a bit of caution in pursuing her own teaching style. Who wants to get their ass whupped?

Thank you, Jimmy James. I owe you one. •

In Joel Stegall's childhood home, words were valued. His father was a preacher; his mother a storyteller and frustrated writer. At Wake Forest University, Joel wandered into a forgettable assignment as managing editor of the school paper. In his career as a professor and academic administrator, he wrote too many tedious memos and inconsequential academic papers. Since retiring, he spends an inordinate amount of time searching for his writer's voice, hoping occasionally to do something others want to read.

.

Cherry Picking To Feed the Soul

by Kaye Threatt

For 40 years I have been going to the century-old Levering Orchard in Cana, Virginia. It is the largest cherry orchard in the South. It always amazes me that I get the same thrill now as I did when I went the first time. It begins with the drive to Cana, an hour's journey from my house in Winston-Salem, North Carolina. The obligatory stop at the Virginia-Carolina Produce Market on U.S. Hwy 52 offers a brief respite before completing the trip.

Soon I drive up the winding road past the pack house and cautiously make a left turn onto Cherry Orchard Lane. The cherry trees come into view! Next, I see the stack of buckets with an attendant who greets me and gives directions to the proper picking area. Always, always, I read the sign about ladder safety and check my buckets to make sure they have hooks.

Then it's on to the assigned picking area. For some unknown reason I have an urgency to start picking right away, afraid that all the cherries will be gone before I can get to the designated spot. While driving down the meandering dirt lane, I want to

Cherry Picking To Feed the Soul

stick my hand out the window and pick a cherry from the car. Yes, some of the trees really are that close. Invariably I will spot an indigo bunting taking flight or hear the croak of a bullfrog. Either makes me keenly aware I'm not alone in my fondness for this setting.

As I drive slowly through the orchard, I am pleased to see the old trees are still bearing fruit, but many new trees are also getting started. This is a sign of an enduring cycle. It's symbolic of the orchard passing from Ralph Levering to his son Sam and on to grandson Frank, the current orchardist. Frank embraces that long tradition and has started another of his own when the cherry-picking is done.

After parking, I change into boots (a necessity for tramping through ubiquitous poison oak—yikes!—and climbing those frighteningly tall ladders). The fun is about to begin. I scamper off to find the tree with the sweetest cherries. Then I realize there are no bad cherries! Up the ladder I climb, step after step until I see the warning, "Don't go beyond this rung!" I love starting at the top and picking my way down the ladder, sometimes turning around with my back to the rungs and getting those cherries that I purposely missed on the ascent. I'm always grateful to catch sight of a ladder man making his rounds, offering to adjust the ladder and thanking me for coming to the orchard. I should be thanking him!

Being in the treetop with only the birds vying for the juiciest cherries is my idea of heaven. I can peer out and marvel at the beauty of the Blue Ridge Mountains. I can hear conversations below me. Sometimes there is talk of what to do with all these cherries. Freeze them? Can them? Dry them? Often the chatter turns into a recipe swap. I love listening to the different accents—some foreign, some local, some hard to understand, but all providing a cultural exchange. Cherry picking is an outing for all ages and ethnic groups. Many times I've wished for my camera to take a photo of an octogenarian picking cherries from the ground or a little child wearing a cherry-stained shirt. We pickers are different in many ways, but we are alike in our love for this little wondrous fruit, filled with antioxidants.

With my buckets brimming with cherries, I head toward the pack house. I pass rusted-out vehicles looking as old as the orchard itself; they seem to point the way to checkout. Again, I know the drill: stand in line, glance at cookbooks for sale, and answer other customers' questions about what I'll do with "all those cherries." As I wait for the next available friendly cashier, I am intrigued by my surroundings. The ghostly pack house is dark and cool with the distinctive smell of fermenting fruit. It houses ancient wooden bins used for harvests long ago. I can imagine this place bustling with workers and buyers alike in its heyday. Suddenly, I'm jolted back to the present, pay up, and start the journey home. This outing never disappoints; it feeds my soul.

Frank Levering was formerly a screen writer in California and has brought that creative side to these mountains through the Cherry Orchard Theater. When the cherry season ends, the theater begins. For years Frank has written and directed plays depicting the local Southern culture. Play-goers arrive with picnic suppers, bottles of wine, and lawn chairs. They head for the hills to enjoy live entertainment under the stars, once again feeding their souls. •

Kaye Threatt lives in Winston-Salem, North Carolina. During her career as a second grade teacher, she most enjoyed giving creative writing assignments, encouraging her students to have their voices be heard in their words. In early retirement, she co-edited the Reynolda House Museum of Art newsletter. Her hobbies include hiking, duplicate bridge, travel and quilting. Her story, "Seasoned Hikers," appeared in the 2019 Personal Essay Publishing Project, *Exploring*.

Flying South

by Patricia Joslin

Nature plays tricks on us sometimes, leaving us to wonder about the predictability of life.

The Minnesota blizzard of 1991 dropped nearly 29 inches of heavy, wet snow in the 48 hours that began on Halloween night. We were there, tromping through the messiness with our 8-year-old eager for treats, carrying a plastic pumpkin. We were young then, long ago. Though Minnesota is a seasonal wonderland, it does require youthful stamina to live there.

Nine-month winters often bring sadness, when daylight wanes and gray skies cloud brains, when frigid winds take breath away and bundled children become caricatures of the Pillsbury Doughboy or the Michelin Tire Man. Families tend to hunker down in winter, with little opportunity to build community beyond the home-castle walls. Fledgling friendships are forged over hot chocolate at the skating rink or in the bleachers at basketball games.

Life in Minnesota revolved around our children and their activities. Daycare, then school events evolved into ball games and prom nights. Homework, housework, and yard work consumed our days. We loved every moment of it. My husband especially relished each moment with our children, whether it was shooting hoops on the driveway, watching the school performance of a gangly teen, or counseling "life-or-death"-seeming decisions about college.

Ten years later, we pondered life as empty-nesters, ready to fly south permanently. Minnesota winters had taken their toll. Retirement golf without donning thermal underwear and earmuffs sounded most appealing. Trips to the mountains or the beach would give us options for exploration. To design and build our dream home with views of verdant woods and orange-pink sunsets over the river sealed the deal. In 2002, with no ties to bind us, we migrated south to the promised land of North Carolina.

The early years in our new habitat fulfilled dreams of quiet beauty and peace. We learned the names of trees in the woodland: tulip poplar, wild black cherry, mockernut hickory, and the obnoxious sweet gum. Red clay, amended by compost, brought forth color, delight, and food for the goldfinches, hummingbirds, and deer. The summer evening chorus of tree frogs and cicadas lulled us into restful sleep. We grew to love this Eden where neighborhood friendships seemed to blossom overnight, and April promised sunshine and blue skies.

Our next ten years in the South were blissful. Days on the golf course were interspersed among volunteer days at the food pantry. I worked in the garden. He built a blog to chronicle his wisdom and espouse his particularly liberal political point-of-view. Brief day trips to Asheville one month, and to Charleston the next, extended into weeks at the beach, often with family. We traveled the world together; we lived life fully.

More importantly, neighborhood friendships deepened each year, becoming bonds built to last a lifetime. The roof leaks? Call John. A new recipe? Call Sarah. New closet shelves? Call Mike. Yoga? Call Jenni. A party? Call everyone! Backyard barbeques, Panther parties on game days, evenings with a glass of wine galvanized our friendships. The circle expanded with each new family who built a home in our neighborhood.

As we began our second decade of Southern living, we searched for the church connectedness we were missing. We looked for a just-right fit. One church, near our home, professed love but fostered exclusion. Another required jacket and tie for him—a non-starter. The just-right place spoke of inclusion for all, outreach to city-wide neighbors, and world missions. We eventually committed to a just-right, vibrant community of believers—just in time.

My husband was healthy then, walking the golf course carrying his clubs. But before the year ended, the diagnosis of pancreatic cancer rocked our foundation. Nature had played its nasty trick, at a too-young age. We needed faith-based support to face the future. Fortunately, during the two-year journey towards death we were sustained, encouraged, and blessed by this congregation's Southern hospitality and by their loving, intimate friendships.

Flying South

95

In the South, we found the covenant of friendship begins with a hug or a strong handshake. Shared stories and shared meals fortify those friendships. Shared laughter and shared tears cement those relationships. Underlying all is the wisdom to acknowledge that we are blessed to be a blessing to others.

He died in May, when Carolina skies were brilliantly blue. I left our bedroom to cry in the sunshine on the back porch while he left our home through the front door, no longer in pain. His promise of love and support was true to the end, as was mine. Now others promised to care for me, love me, hold me close. Though we migrated south for the weather, we stayed for the warmth of community, and the promise of hope and happiness.

And now alone, I know that flying south is coming home. •

Patricia Joslin lives in Charlotte, North Carolina, where she mingles with other new writers at Charlotte Lit. Reared in the Midwest, she learned to brave the winters but now prefers to spend her days under Carolina blue skies. Dr. Joslin is a retired educator who has published professionally. She has journaled for over 30 years, dabbled in poetry, and now participates in a writing group affiliated with Levine Cancer Institute. This is her first creative nonfiction publication.

The Cause of the Trouble
by Randell Jones

I was older when I first married and my wife a good bit
younger. It's worked out well for nearly 40 years so far in
part because she's a formidable woman. And she comes
by it honestly as do our daughters, all coming from a long line
of strong Southern women.

In our early married years, when we would visit her mother in
the mountains of North Georgia, my mother-in-law indulged
my curiosity about her growing up in Appalachia. The stories
about Kertie Mae's childhood during the 1930s in Gilmer
County seemed to unfold in circumstances I associated more
with a generation earlier, more like that of my grandparents
who came of age before World War I. In time, I wrote those
stories for posterity blending what she might have said with
what I swear I heard. Yeah, that's on me, but here it is:

> Kertie Mae's mama, Myrtle Bell, didn't teach her much
> different from what she'd learned. Mytle Bell had it
> rough as a child since her daddy had been killed right
> in front of her eyes at age five and her mother had
> reared the children alone. Maybe Myrtle thought

making her kids tough was the only way to help them survive. And maybe it was. Kertie remembered one time she sassed her mama in the kitchen, and Myrtle came across her back with a chunk of stovewood the size of your forearm. Kertie flew across the room and hit the wall. After a while she was able to catch her breath, but she'd already got the message, she said. Love was earned around there. Nothing was free.

Despite Myrtle's temper, Kertie begged to go to school. Back then, people didn't see much point in educating a girl, Kertie said. A woman needed to know how to cook and can and quilt. The rest of it was just extra stuff for folks not like her family to mess with. Other folks had time and money; her family had chores and children. And Myrtle Bell didn't want Kertie going to school because she was afraid the boys would get after her. The way Kertie was raised though, she was ill as a hornet and would have slapped the fire out of any boy who even looked at her wrong. Soon enough she got her chance.

Kertie was 13 and in the fifth grade in a one-room school. Mr. Waldo Brookshire taught everybody the same stuff at the same time, and the students had to catch on as best they could. Kertie was only going part of the year anyway since she had so much to do on the farm.

One day, she recalled, a man rode by the schoolhouse on a mule and Mr. Brookshire stopped class so he could go outside and speak to him. Mr. Brookshire warned the students to behave while he was gone. He wasn't too far outside, Kertie said, when Clyde Hyde, who was younger than she and about 10 years old, jumped up from his desk and scurried over to hers. He stood there for a second, then looked down at Kertie, pointed at her chest and said, "titty." Before he knew what was happening, she grabbed his ears, one in each hand, and nearly wrung them off his head with him hollering for her to let go. She glanced out the window in time to see Mr. Brookshire starting back inside. She let go of Clyde's ears, figuring he'd got the message.

Mr. Brookshire wanted to know what all the commotion was about. Nobody said a word. He kept asking the class to confess what they'd been up to. He was getting madder every second nobody would tell. Finally, Myrtle Cantrell blurted the whole thing out and then everybody was mad at her, Kertie declared. Mr. Brookshire sent everybody outside to play except her and Clyde. She wasn't sure what he was going to do, but lucky for him he'd decided only to give them a talking to. The whole time he was grumbling, she said, she had her eye on a big piece of firewood over by the stove just in case he even thought about trying to spank her.

In time we figured out the truth behind the story about Myrtle Bell seeing her father killed, shot down in the yard by Tobe Chastain. It was not the story we expected. It seems Myrtle Bell's daddy and Tobe had some bad blood between them. A

The Cause of the Trouble

newspaper clipping from 1898 told the tale. It seems Myrtle Bell's daddy "had cut Tobe's thoat (*sic*) but had not finished the job, and that was the cause of the trouble between them."

And so it's gone, generation after generation: strong women, foolish men—including this writer who might well soon discover he is the cause of his own trouble. •

Randell Jones is an award-winning history writer about the pioneer and Revolutionary War eras. Since 2007, he has served as an invited member of the Road Scholars Speakers Bureau of the North Carolina Humanities Council. He created the Personal Story Publishing Project and the companion podcast, "6-minute Stories," to encourage writers. He lives in Winston-Salem, North Carolina. His wife is a CPA, Chartered Financial Analyst, Certified Financial Planner, a marvelous cook, and lucky for him a very forgiving soul.

Living in the South
by Bill Donohue

I grew up in America's heartland, awash with a bag of
stereotypes and bias against pretty much anyone who
didn't sound like Walter Cronkite or behave like Mary
Tyler Moore.

I remember my first cultural comeuppance following a move
to New York where my biases were embarrassingly transparent:
People in the East were aloof and cold, and Jewish. Not only
did I find it embarrassingly untrue—new friends were easy to
acquire and altogether lovely in countenance—I was met with
the notion that people on that side of the continent held
strange opinions about Midwesterners. What? you say!

> "You know, moving to Iowa, you can't even unpack
> before some do-gooder neighbor is at your front door
> with a tater tot casserole wondering if you've always
> been Methodist."

Struck dumb with the assault, I nearly burst out with
"sometimes we also bring Jell-O salads." The reality that we are

by geographic nature and strong parenting altogether kind, warm, and generous—and a lot of other things—somehow didn't register. Hadn't they read anything by Garrison Keillor?

Not long after that I attended a writers' workshop where Jill McCorkle introduced me to "woulda, coulda, shoulda." While her writing also introduced other forms of Southern humanity and even humor, I was mostly left curious. As fate would have it, I moved, with apprehension and curiosity, to Winston-Salem where I confronted my Southern biases head-on: not so smart, slow, Confederate, shoeless, squirrel hunters—you know, hillbillies. We quickly noted the absence of Jell-O molds and smiled politely with the slow talkers. They wore shoes, of course, and talked in full sentences, but what struck me face-on was the unapologetic, unbridled theological evangelism with nearly every welcome query: "You're new; where do you worship? Found a church yet?" Over time I learned it was a sweet concern that I find a social anchor here in the South, a touchstone of the community, not a lead-up invitation to tent revivals.

My wife and I morphed, over time, from occasional and moderately curious church goers to bona fide regulars, simultaneously wrapped in the warmth and political tutoring of the quilters—the acknowledged keepers of the faith and all associated rumors and folklore of the tribe. We became just other pilgrims in the endless pews of advocacy and concern, trying to listen more deeply, seek justice on every street corner and build community in the absence of racial or gender or cultural harmony.

Blessedly, our tater-tot casseroles were accepted without reservation, our adopted Korean daughter was married in the fellowship hall under the "Tree of Life" and our son with Down syndrome now offers communion with his fiancé each month. We have a new home, an extended family—the anchor to the community that the slow-talking people trumpeted to us, in their own musical way.

Not long ago I visited my daughter in Korea where there were no casseroles, but also seemingly no homeless. Unlike Iowa or New York or North Carolina, there was also, and most curiously, no eye contact. Therein lies the key, I've found. I hadn't known enough about Korea to build up any real appreciation or bias about eye contact. I was merely curious. At the same time, I observed another cultural phenomenon: everyone held hands! On the streets, in the metro, everywhere. Classmates, friends, family of all ages and genders—affectionate, but asexual. I'm sure I harbored deeply buried World War II biases, something about slanted eyes and kamikaze fighters. Even though my rational mind could differentiate Korea from Japan, there were probably some neuro transmissions I was unaware of. But I was curious about hand-holding and eye contact, and that was the key: curiosity trumps judgement. A curious soul is an open, learning soul.

So even though the South and the church and the absence of Mary Tyler Moore were troublesome to hard-wired, heartland instincts, it was curiosity which emerged as my bellwether.

Biases and stereotypes can be harsh and unintentionally cruel. NPR says they are almost impossible to extinguish. But the malicious pair melt pretty easily when approached with a dose of humanity and curiosity.

In South Dakota, we learned that you don't lock your front door when you leave home—someone might need to get in! Blizzards kill! In Massachusetts, we learned that everyone wasn't a Kennedy Catholic; there were even Republican Episcopalians on Cape Cod.

Some universal totems of neighborliness span all cultures. We have things in common, although ones not always obvious on first glance. Sure, you need to keep your doors unlocked in South Dakota winters. And in both North Carolina and Iowa you are smart to lock your car doors in August. Otherwise your back seat fills up with zucchini!

Whoda, coulda, shoulda thought it? •

Dr. William Donohue and his family live in Winston Salem where they advocate for all families with disabilities and chronic illness. Bill published *The Kind of September: A Race Against Time and Alzheimer's* in 2013.

From the Heart in Dixie
by Beth Sammons

Northern Alabama is not simply my birthplace, it is the landscape that provided my earliest learnings about life, limits and love. It is a layered rose, pretty to see, but whose petals are fragile and hiding prickly thorns. It is the Deep South where language is both respectful and demeaning, where fiery love and hate coexist.

I was born in 1958 and reared in Hartselle, a self-proclaimed Christian town filled with an abundance of Southern charm, football worshippers, and George C. Wallace lovers. We also had a few unconventional white families and persevering black families who showed one another mutual respect.

From the time I was three years old, my two sisters and I stood a deathwatch over our chronically ill mother. During the years-long vigil, she represented for me an authentic Christian and strong Southern woman. I still hear Mama's soft Alabama accent as I picture her affectionate smile and sparkling black eyes that danced as she story talked. Mama's hands moved in rhythm to punctuate every word within her creative stories that mesmerized her children and husband, even during our most fearful and anxious times. Her former school students told us about Mama's fun and creative ways of teaching lessons in English and History. In our church, adults lined up to attend her Sunday school class when she felt well enough to teach. She was a force. She had power. She could change hearts.

Before Mama's petite frame became overpowered by invasive bladder cancer and a degenerative kidney disease, she often put me on her hip and strolled around the yard, introducing me to the sweet scent of magnolia blossoms, honeysuckle, and flowering wisteria. We watched the pesky squirrels quarrel with the beautiful birds, bees, and butterflies. I listened. I learned. Nature became my safe haven in the scariest of years to come.

While Mama spent long bouts in the hospital, I cherished my time with Papa. He'd take me to his cabin at Spring Creek. We'd visit with the neighbors who I called Uncle Richard, Aunt Mary, and their daughter, Miss Bea. They worried over Mama's illness and wanted to make sure Papa and I ate "plenty good," serving us the best barbeque, fried catfish, greens and cornbread ever made along the Tennessee River.

Richard and Bea took me fishing along the creek bed and showed me the proper way to pick blackberries and to pick cotton. My fun distractions left Papa free to consume his blended whiskey which he used as an escape from his plethora of fears, responsibilities, and uncertainties. Mama didn't worry about Papa and me near as much when we went to the cabin as she did when we went to the VFW. She knew Richard and his family would watch over us, especially when we three girls had no other Christian friends or relatives who offered to keep us while Mama fought to live and Papa fought to pay the mounting medical bills.

After I turned 12, the rest of my world caved in, for it was Papa's weakened heart and body that could no longer survive, instead of Mama's. Papa died in the hospital parking lot with my frail Mama and frightened middle sister by his side. The emergency room staff had refused treatment for Papa because he could not afford medical insurance.

At Papa's funeral, my sisters and I huddled beside Mama in the front row of the church. Papa's death broke Mama's spirit as no illness could. We sat silent in our pain, until a commotion made us jerk around. Standing in the entryway was a wide-eyed Richard with his gentlemen's hat in one hand and Mary and Bea clinging to his arm. We could hear the ushers' voices. They were in a heated discussion over who was going to seat them in the balcony as there had never been any "colored people" in our church. Mama raised her frail body from her seat, stood erect, and motioned for Richard and his family to join us in the front pew. The congregation sat stone-still as Richard, Mary and Bea walked cautiously up the aisle focusing only on Mama's fiery black eyes, which then cooled and began to sparkle and dance with gratitude, respect, and unconditional love. She stood firm, facing the congregation until the three were seated safely with us. Mama's actions said everything that needed to be said. The tension hung in the air for another few moments and then dissipated as the service began.

The Deep South is filled with caring, colorful, and contra-dictive characters who taught me how to be genuine, merciful,

From the Heart in Dixie

and tolerant. But from the heart in Dixie came the bone-deep love Mama offered as she showed us that we have within us everything needed to heal and to forgive and to grow. •

Beth Sammons lives on the outskirts of Eureka Springs, Arkansas, a charming Victorian village filled with colorful artists, musicians and writers. She is a member of The Village Writing School, Holiday Island Art Guild, and the Reader Writer Group. Recently, Beth has become an ambitious creative writer who tells real and raw stories in a compelling way to engage the reader. She is currently writing a collection of personal essays and memoirs for magazine submissions and ultimately to compile a book.

.

Empty Pocketbook, Boundless Love
by Debra Madaris Efird

Mamaw, I called her. We were quite close, for grand-mothers played a weighty role in raising children in small Southern towns in the 1960s. During summers I'd spend countless weeks firmly entrenched at her ramshackle house, seeing my parents only rarely. My grandfather, Papaw, was there, but his alcoholism kept him in the background and defined his impact negatively. The undisputed attraction was Mamaw, a pint-sized dynamo with an empty pocketbook but expansive wealth.

Mamaw's house was a kid's paradise—almost no rules! When my cousins visited, we'd jump on the beds, experiment with Mamaw's Avon perfumes, and play "shoe store" with her size 4 shoes. She presented all of us with stacks of clothes she'd sewn during the winter months from remnants bought at the five-and-dime. Simple crop tops and elastic-waist shorts had us strutting as if we were Paris fashion models.

Mamaw claimed she didn't care for cats, but somehow every summer a new litter of kittens was born under the porch to some stray she'd started feeding. I always believed she arranged this pleasure just for me.

She stocked a generous supply of sweets from the nearby Merita outlet, which sold day-old baked goods at a discount. The path to the little store was kept worn down by our near-daily visits to buy honey buns, raisin cakes, and powdered sugar doughnuts. The downside was that my dentist never failed to find cavities.

The only work required of me was to help pick vegetables in the garden. In a jiffy we'd fill several large buckets of produce, some to be shared with neighbors but most making its way to her table. Staple foods of the South—green beans, stewed squash, fried okra, and fluffy biscuits—satisfied us. Occasionally there was "meat"—Vienna sausages! Thick slices of tomato and cucumber were her dessert, though I favored those powdery doughnuts.

When evening arrived, Mamaw and I preferred sitting on the front porch to watching television. Sometimes we'd read magazines by the yellow porch light or pore over fat Sears' catalogs, taking turns choosing our favorite outfit on each page. When the noisy fumigator truck barreled through the streets spraying for mosquitos, we clapped our hands, totally unaware of the toxicity of the fog we inhaled.

For many years I didn't realize she was poor, though the signs were surely there. The kitchen had no sink—only a faucet out on the back porch. For hot water, Mamaw had to heat a pot on the stove. Drinking water was kept in a bucket with a communal dipper. The rest of us felt sorry for one cousin whose very-particular mother spoke of "germs" and wouldn't let her take a swig from it.

Long past the days when most people used a standard toilet, we trekked to a creepy outhouse in the backyard or, at night, relieved ourselves in a bedside chamber pot. When I was eight, the city condemned the outhouse, and the landlord was required to build a small bathroom onto the back porch. The addition had no heat, but at least we could flush away our "business," and we had a little sink for washing hands. Baths still took place in large, tin tubs on the floor of the kitchen— the same tubs we washed vegetables in by day. Mamaw seemed to think I needed a bath only once or twice a week, a sweet secret I kept from my parents.

When we went downtown, we rode in a taxicab. Such adventure! We walked the mile to church, even in rain. The inconvenience and dependency created by the lack of a car was lost on me.

The house was full of vermin. The mice didn't scare me as much as the insects. Mamaw protected me by swatting wasps that found their way through holes in screens and circled above like vultures. And when I pointed out to her the roaches that brazenly skimmed the floor at night, they faced the same fierce treatment.

However, one problem my seemingly invincible Mamaw could not squash: Papaw's drunkenness. She tried to minimize his binge-drinking by calling it "celebrating," but his steady stream of profanity was anything but joyful. When he shouted explicit threats, we'd hurry into her bedroom. She'd latch the door and assure me we were safe while he banged away with his fists on the other side. Then came the day I witnessed him chasing her around the table with a butcher knife, and my already strained regard for Papaw was forever shattered.

Somehow Mamaw survived these scenarios, and I moved on. What she couldn't provide me in physical comforts, she supplemented with a boundless reserve of love. I learned young that life's vermin don't matter so much if you've had a hero show you how to swat them. •

Debra Madaris Efird lives in Harrisburg, North Carolina, and is a member of the NC Writers' Network. She is author of the book *Groups in Practice: A School Counselor's Collection* (Routledge, 2012). Her writing has appeared in professional counseling magazines, *saturdayeveningpost.com*, *livinglutheran.org*, *Savannah Anthology*, *Wake Living* magazine, *UNCG* magazine, and other venues. Most recently she was awarded First Prize in The Writers Workshop of Asheville 2019 Literary Fiction Contest. Like many writers, she claims it's a great day only if she is writing.

Why Do Things Have To Be So Hard
by Lubrina Burton

The last place I thought I would find myself thinking about my home in Southeastern Kentucky was at the Night Infiltration Course in Basic Training at Ft. Leonard Wood, Missouri on a hot, sticky July evening in 1997. I was wondering if I'd actually be able to crawl the 150 meters under prickly concertina wire with my unwieldy rucksack and M-16 while the Army shot off live tracer rounds and flares over my head. I'd scarcely stopped shaking even when the drill sergeants screamed at us to hit the dirt. My helmet shoved my oversized Army-Issued "Birth Control Glasses" off my face somewhere along the route. But I counted myself lucky that I still had my britches on when I stood up at the end since I'd been certain I was going to lose them, too.

After finishing the course, I met up with my comrades in the black, Missouri forest. I threw my rucksack alongside the other packs on the ground. The soldiers were sitting around their gear with their Kevlar helmets off. The drill sergeants either didn't care or didn't notice in the darkness that we were being so lax, and I quickly followed suit. Finally, a moment to breathe. Man, that was hard.

Basic was now almost over. I would be a soldier soon! I was 17 years old, fresh off my junior year in high school, and the first woman in my family to join the military.

I sat on my rucksack, dangling my helmet by its chinstrap. I stared up at the stars as the cannons blasted out their man-made meteors, lighting up the Midwestern sky. It was one of the most beautiful sights I had ever seen. A tear fell into the hollowness of my Kevlar. I thought about a different evening back home when I sat on the porch with my two beagles looking up at the Kentucky heavens contemplating my decision to join the Army. I wanted to be a soldier, I told myself then. It was my choice. But I often wondered, Why do things have to be so hard?

In school, teachers told us, "Boys, don't go down in the mines. The coal companies robbed us and made us serfs on our own land. You can do something different. Girls, if y'all wanna be teachers, know there are only so many schools in this county. You kids need to leave here if you want good jobs. It'll be hard, but y'all will have to do it."

My mom left home only to return from Cincinnati after divorcing my violent father when I was four. She often told me, "A woman has to take care of herself. If I'd stayed with your dad, he woulda done killed me by now."

Mom was able to raise my brother and me in her hometown by driving two hours away to work as a nurse in a Lexington hospital on weekends, pulling doubles just to make ends meet. She was proud that she was able to afford to get us out of a leaky, single-wide trailer up a "holler" and into a brick ranch closer to town. But it was hard on all of us.

"I've sacrificed for you since you were born, and I did it all on my own," Mom declared. "And you'll have to make it on your own. I'm done raisin' you after you turn eighteen," she plainly told me that spring. I was college-bound with good grades, but not good enough for scholarships. With no money and no skills, how would I manage all alone? The Army with the GI Bill would be my ticket out.

On that night before I left for Basic, I pulled my dogs in close and sobbed into their soft fur. Part of me still wanted one more summer to be a kid, play with my pups, and dream up at the sky. But it was time to grow up, leave home, and become a woman.

Back in Missouri, the drill sergeants called for us to get into formation. The cannons were letting up and it was time to head out. I stood up and inhaled the humid air mixed with the dry dirt. I had grown accustomed not only to the feeling, but I had started to enjoy the slight pain the odd mixture brought to my lungs. With each burning breath I was closer to the life I wanted.

I breathed the scorched air into my chest and exhaled my doubts. I looked over my shoulder to catch one last glimpse of the awesome tracers. Then I slung my rucksack onto my back, picked up my M16, and marched off—ready to face the next hard things to come. •

Lubrina Burton resides in Lexington, Kentucky and hails from rural Knox County. She credits her second-grade teacher and cousin, Ms. Thelma Buell, for first encouraging and nurturing her love of writing. Lubrina is a veteran of the U.S. Army and a graduate of Eastern Kentucky University. Currently she is enrolled in the Carnegie Center's Author Academy in Lexington. She is working on a collection of personal essays related to her time in the military.

Mom, You Did What!
by Suzanne Cottrell

E scargot? I wasn't sure how to pronounce it let alone how to eat them. My parents had surprised me with a "Sweet Sixteen" birthday dinner at an upscale restaurant. Pizza would have made me happy. My cheeks flushed as I watched my parents insert miniature forks into the steamed shells, twist and withdraw snails, then dip them into melted, garlic butter. I gagged and excused myself from the table.

Now that my daughter was in high school, I recalled that incident. I didn't want her to feel uncomfortable or embarrassed with the upcoming Country Club social engagements and high school junior prom. One evening when we were doing the dishes, I said, "Molly, I've enrolled you in Cotillion classes."

"You did what!" screamed Molly.
"You heard me. I registered you for Cotillion classes."
"Without asking me?" Molly stomped her foot.
"I knew you'd say no. You'll thank me later."
"Ugh, right," Molly huffed.

Mom, You Did What!

117

"They teach you proper manners and ballroom dancing."

"You're kidding, right?" Molly said.

"You'll have fun. You love to dress up and go to parties."

"Why can't you teach me?" Molly pleaded.

"That's not a good idea. You get an attitude whenever I correct you. Besides think of this as a Southern rite of passage into womanhood," I said.

"I thought that happened with my period," replied Molly.

"Molly, that's not very lady-like. The first class is next Thursday night."

I should have read the fine print: "Parents/Guardians are expected to participate and model proper manners and basic dance techniques." *Mmmmmm, I hope I can find my copy of Emily Post's etiquette book. We'll need my mother's complete set of sterling silverware to practice setting a formal table.*

"Molly. Hurry up. We need to go. You don't want to be late your first night."

Molly stood at the top of the stairs dangling the cream-colored tights in her fingers. "Mom, do you really expect me to wear these with that dress?"

I rushed up the stairs and into Molly's room where I saw a sleeveless fuchsia cocktail dress and strappy heels laid out on her bed. "Young lady, did you read the dress code?" I grabbed the crinoline-lined peach dress and handed it to Molly. "Don't forget your gloves."

When we arrived at the community center, the youngsters stood in a receiving line. The instructor, Ms. Amelia Peacock, led the parents in greeting the students with a good evening and firm handshake.

"Molly, run over and get at the end of the line," I urged.

Molly popped a piece of gum in her mouth, grabbed her gloves, and scurried over to the end of the line. She stared at the ground and fidgeted with her hands. When Ms. Peacock arrived, she said, "Young lady, head up. Good evening."

Molly extended her hand and whispered, "Good evening."
"Speak up. Firm handshake. Young lady, spit out that gum."
"Where?" Molly asked.
"Here. Take this tissue." Ms. Peacock slapped a tissue in Molly's hand.

Molly turned slightly, spit her gum into the tissue, and balled it up. I walked up behind her and took the tissue as discreetly as I could. Molly glared at me.

Once inside, Ms. Peacock and her assistants directed the adolescents to their assigned seats, boy-girl, boy-girl. Each place was set for a formal dinner with nine utensils. Molly raised her eyebrows. The napkin folded on the center of the plate looked like an origami swan.

"Young ladies and gentlemen, this evening you will learn the proper placement and usage of these utensils. Pay attention," Ms. Peacock commanded. She gently shook out her napkin and placed it in her lap. She proceeded with lengthy explanations.

I saw Molly nudge the boy seated to her left and ask him something. I imagine his mom registered him for classes too.

Mom, You Did What!

On the way home, Molly said, "Mom, I'm never going to remember which fork to use."

"Rule of thumb: start with the one farthest from the plate and work inward with each course," I said. *At least I remembered that much.* "Then use your common sense. You'll be all right. We can practice at home. You'll be ready for the graduation ceremony and the ball in seven weeks."

Graduation night Molly wore a beautiful, white, laced gown, cream-colored tights, long white gloves, and satin pumps. After watching the initial awkwardness of Molly and her classmates, I smiled as she dined and danced like a reluctant, budding debutante. At some point, Molly left her friends for a moment and hurried over to me. In a confident voice and with a warm hug, she said, "Thanks Mom."

Tears welled in my eyes. I looked around for Ms. Peacock. *Where is a tissue when you need one?* •

Suzanne Cottrell, a member of the Granville County Writers' Group and NC Writers' Network, lives with her husband and three rescue dogs in rural Granville County, North Carolina. An outdoor enthusiast and retired teacher, she enjoys reading, writing, knitting, hiking, Pilates, and Tai Chi. Her prose has appeared in numerous journals and anthologies, including *Bearing Up*, *Exploring*, *Pop Machine*, *Unwanted Visitors*, *Empty Silos*, *Dragon Poet Review*, *Dual Coast Magazine*, *Parks and Points*, and *Nailpolish Stories, A Tiny and Colorful Literary Journal*.

Her Dusty Road to a Life of Service
by Phyliss Grady Adcock

My mother was reared in a dysfunctional home with an alcoholic father. Life was scary, unpredictable, void of fun, and always embarrassing. The four children were never sure where the next meal would come from, when they would have to leave home unexpectedly, and what their father might do in public. The constant needs for clothing and basic items for school were continuing reminders that they were at the bottom.

My grandmother had little time for nurturing, playing with her children. She took every part time job to bring in enough money to keep things going. She did laundry, mended clothes, scrubbed floors, and did work on farms where she could take her children along. Life was a battle, and she was the only soldier fighting. With this childhood upbringing, a young girl might be ill equipped to be a good mother, much less an exceptional one. But life gives us trials to teach us great lessons. My mother was surely an A+ student in the school of hard knocks.

School was my mother's worst nightmare. Her shoes and socks had holes in them. She walked a mile to school down a dusty road in those sad shoes, carrying her homemade lunch. Other children ridiculed her. She remembered being clean but never quite "presentable." Her classmates confirmed that self-image of a pitiful, thrown away little girl. Teachers, too, treated her in accordance with how she looked. She couldn't possibly be smart, they reasoned, if her parents sent her to school so poorly cared for.

My mother's left-handedness was regarded as a genetic mistake in the 1930s. Her arm was tied to her seat most of first grade to train her to use the "proper" hand. When she was untied and reverted immediately to her left hand, she was locked in the closet at school. Forgotten by the teacher, she was retrieved only later from the dark after not returning home. Back then, no one saw my mother's brilliance, creativity, and passion for others. That was too well hidden beneath hand-me-down clothes.

As a mother in her own time, she made sure her children never felt the shame she had. Our childhoods were magical. She became the model "grade mother" all classes wished for, making sure every child in the class felt special, cared for, and loved. Through her church, she made sure every child in our neighborhood felt invited. Indeed, throughout my childhood, I saw her look out for needy children and offer her best.

In her seventies, she began managing Martha's Mission Food Pantry in Morehad City, North Carolina, to help people struggling to feed their families. She garnered financial support for this mission from communities across the county. She personally served on-call after hours delivering groceries and diapers to a young mother abandoned in a motel room and purchased a fan for a child enduring cancer treatments and having no air-conditioning. She convinced proud fishermen, during a red tide, that accepting food from the pantry did not reflect on their work ethic or their roles as providers for their families; these grateful men later refilled the pantry freezers with seafood they had harvested.

My mother's compassion extended beyond the stated mission of the pantry, she on occasion using her own money to make sure no child went hungry. She was challenged once that a mother requesting food was undeserving because her husband gambled away his pay each week. My mother declared that the children had no control over their father's actions, but she did have control over providing help for children who needed food. Knowing the needs from her own childhood, she worked diligently to see that no child went hungry because of bad circumstances and poor choices by others.

My mother's work was rewarded at times in loving hugs on the street from people she had helped. They were just God's sheep and very grateful to a caring woman who did not judge them because of what they needed. She had walked many miles in their shoes as a child.

My mother, Anna Richardson Grady Coleman, was recognized, in time, by a larger community grateful for her service. In 2000, she was honored among a select group of volunteering citizens from across North Carolina with the distinguished

Governor's Service Award. What a surprise it was to a grown woman who still looked in the mirror each morning and saw a struggling child trying to be "enough." She was transformed in her life into much more than "enough," we know. She was "enough" to rescue children who were victims of this world and of difficult and challenging family circumstances.

Much beauty and goodness grew from my mother's beginning journey down that dry, dirt path with holes in her shoes. She walked that road mindful of her blessings into a life of love and service to others. •

Phyliss Grady Adcock retired from teaching and lives in Morehead City, North Carolina. She has been published in *Mailbox Magazine* and *Teacher's Helper*. Her current writing is a story of Alzheimer's from a child's point of view and a collection of inspirational stories.

Southern Blues

by Janet K. Baxter

We moved from Wisconsin to Brookhaven, Mississippi, in 1978. We had good times and fun memories and stories of our time in Brookhaven; however, three disquieting events there markedly affected me as a young woman.

At that time, the South had endured over two decades of social unrest from civil rights activism and Supreme Court decisions that supported the rights of African-American citizens by integrating communities and desegregating the public schools. The United Klans of America (that is, the Ku Klux Klan, the KKK) was active across the United States. Pictures of robed members appeared in local and national newspapers. The organization terrorized African-American citizens, businesses, and churches. Catholics, Jews, Muslims, and aliens were included in their rhetoric.

This move transplanted our small family into the center of lingering social and cultural tensions. My husband, Michael, was transferred specifically to integrate the industrial plant in Brookhaven. The local community did not relish this change.

Although overt aggression against "Northerners" did not occur in Brookhaven while we lived there, the more subtle attacks of resentment and rejection seemed to be skillfully directed at the wives and children.

One young woman moved to Brookhaven at the same time we did. Our husbands worked together, and we socialized at company picnics and holiday dinners. We were each pregnant with our second children at the same time; we struck up a friendship. She and her husband were Mississippians and she was quickly accepted into the community, joining the local sorority for young, white, married women. Kindly, she extended an invitation to me to join the sorority and I, socially starved, gladly accepted.

Each sorority member was paired with a "secret sister" for one year; we were to send cards or small gifts for birthdays and anniversaries. I was diligent. Since this was my first experience in a sorority, I didn't want to be slack. One year, the secret sister with whom I was paired never sent a card for the entire year. She did admit, however, at the last meeting when secret sister pairings were revealed that she was embarrassed.
I wondered. Was she really embarrassed? Was this an accidental slight from an overwhelmed young mother or was this covert rejection? I'll never know for sure, but I do remember being confused and disappointed that she would forget me all year.

During the same period, the refugee crises following the end of the Vietnam War was constantly in the news. We saw live images broadcasted on television and graphic pictures appeared on the front page of local newspapers. My husband

and I were drawn to this crisis on a personal level as we watched refugee families with young children like ours be found adrift in small boats fleeing the country. We decided to answer the plea from Catholic Charities based in Jackson, Mississippi. They were looking for foster parents to take in unaccompanied Vietnamese minors held in refugee camps.

One memory from this experience during our time in Brookhaven most knifes through my heart. It was when we brought our refugee foster children, Ha and Thinh, home to join our family. I had been so excited when we were approved to be permanent-foster parents through the Catholic Charities Unaccompanied Minors Program. I shared my excitement with the sorority; I was so proud. Other sorority sisters had added children to their families. We celebrated these births with baby showers. Sisters would share maternity clothes and offer children's clothing. But, after we brought our children home even after months of waiting, I received not a card nor a note of congratulations, not a hug or shouts of excitement. No one offered hand-me-downs, so much needed as both children had few clothes. We were left to celebrate alone.

We had multiple reasons for leaving Mississippi in 1985, but one memorable incident hastened our departure. We were driving through Jackson on a main thoroughfare with our children in the car. At one corner, robed and hooded Klansmen were shouting and holding signs facing the traffic as we passed. Being Catholic and with two Vietnamese refugee children in the back seat, this sight sent a shock of fear through me. I can't tell you exactly what I was thinking: I needed to protect Ha and Thinh from the brutalities within

this country which they had suffered so long to reach?
I wanted to protect my birth children, Sarah and Adam, from
seeing and hearing the people who hated us and their new
brother and sister? Did I fear that we were physically at risk?
Did I fear what might happen in the future?

I looked at Michael and declared, "We're moving!"

And we did. •

Janet K. Baxter lives in Kings Mountain, North Carolina and is a
member of the Charlotte Writer's Club. Her story "Horse
Whispering for the Average Woman" appeared in *Exploring*. She
achieved second place in the 2018-2019 Charlotte Writer's Club
Nonfiction Contest. Janet retired as Director of Special Education at
University of North Carolina-Charlotte. She enjoys her grandchildren and all the horses, dogs, and cats that populate her "mini-
estate." Janet's hobbies include horseback riding on local trails,
crocheting, yoga, and letter-writing.

Saying Goodbye
by Howard Pearre

I was already asleep when Mama called me from Wilmington and told me my father had died. She said she was all right and there was no need for me to come down until the weekend.

I took off Friday anyway and got there a little after lunchtime. We cried a little bit and then Mama suggested that we go to a pizza place for something to eat. We went to the restaurant and ate pizza and talked about Daddy and plans for a service after the cremation.

He had been in that nursing home for more than two years. I wouldn't say he was slowly dying, but he certainly wasn't having much fun. Mama lived close by at their apartment in the retirement community. I'd get down every month or two and would try to brighten his day by taking him out for a ride or even to get a pizza and a beer. Daddy had been a skinny kid when he'd served in the Army in India, but he'd enjoyed way too much of Mama's cooking since those days. Our trips out were only moderately successful with me wrestling him in and out of my car and wheelchairs, exhausting both of us.

He was frustrated and tired of living in a bed under harsh florescent lights and with the constant drone of other residents' TV sets. One time, he called me close and looked deeply into my face and said with fierce seriousness, "Why can't a man just go on and die?"

I stumbled for words to give some encouragement to this man who had held my hand crossing streets and pushed me off for my first solo bicycle ride.

"It's just not time, Daddy. It's not up to us," I said. Feeble words. He gazed at me for a moment then sank back into his pillow.

When my sister arrived on Saturday, we had some more tears and held each other. Then I put on the nice clothes I'd brought, and Mama dressed up in her church clothes. We were just going to the funeral home to see Daddy and to sign release papers for the cremation but dressing up seemed to be the thing to do. It was a beautiful crisp blue-sky March morning.

On the way to the funeral home, we made small talk about our children and Daddy and the plans for a burial service later in Charlotte.

As we crossed an intersection, we passed an old service station that had been converted into a day-old bread store.
"Can you turn around, son?" my mother said. "I just remembered. I need a loaf of bread."

I negotiated several turns on Market Street and pulled into the bread store, quickly adjusting from the somber tone of our funeral home mission to that of a shopping trip.

And it wasn't a quick in-and-out—Mama actually shopped. Before she tallied up with the clerk, she'd gathered a loaf of whole wheat, a loaf of rye with seeds, and half a pound cake, something to serve to any friends who might come by the apartment.

At the funeral home, a quiet, smiling man in a suit took us to the lower floor by an elevator. He warned us it might not be pleasant because they don't do any special preparation for a cremation as they would for a funeral service. We said we still wanted to view the body, so he took us into the workroom where Daddy's body, dressed simply in his pajamas, rested on a metal table.

It just came to me what to say.

"This is not Daddy," I said, and my sister and Mama knew exactly what I meant, that the body that was lying on the table in that room was not the man who had been my mother's husband for 56 years, who had taught my sister to roller skate and quizzed me on times tables, who had ushered for years at the Methodist Church, and who had donated gallons of blood to the Red Cross. What we saw on that table was just where Daddy had lived for a long time.

But the funeral director did not know what I meant. A look of panic took the place of his smile. He stuttered.

"I am so . . . I'll . . . I'll have to check the paperwork."

I realized I had confused the poor man and quickly assured him the funeral home had made no mistake.

We went back upstairs to the man's office. We all three read the papers closely, and Mama signed them.

We held each other again and left the funeral home. Then we went back to the apartment where Mama fixed us turkey sandwiches on day-old whole wheat and rye. •

Howard Pearre lives in Winston-Salem, North Carolina. He has published short fiction and memoir essays in *Second Spring* and *Bearing Up* anthologies, and *GreenPrints* magazine. He retired as a manager with NC Vocational Rehabilitation and later as a counselor with the Department of Veterans Affairs. He volunteers at Reynolda Gardens, conducts voter registration training workshops, and strives to keep up with six widely-dispersed grandchildren. He is a member of Winston-Salem Writers.

The White Section
by JP McGillicuddy

A month after my 23rd birthday, I jumped into my 1972 Chevy Kingswood and headed from my native Massachusetts to Charlotte, North Carolina. It was my first time venturing into the South and I wasn't sure what I would find. I'd gleaned facts from history classes about the Civil War, Jim Crow laws, and segregation. TV and newspapers also made me aware of Martin Luther King, Jr., civil rights demonstrations, and racial discrimination. But this was 1980, and I'd never heard anything on these topics linked to Charlotte. In fact, the only thing I knew about Charlotte was that a job was waiting for me there as ticket manager for a new professional soccer team in the American Soccer League (ASL).

So, with the ink barely dry on my UMASS diploma, I not only filled a small suitcase with clothes, I also packed a trunk full of Northern, suburban, white-man ignorance about the South. For good measure, I added a helping of naive, self-righteous liberalism. After all, I'd attended high school, played football, partied and hung out with kids of various ethnicities. So, I figured it came down to a "do unto others" philosophy. No sweat, right?

A week into my position as ticket manager, I fielded a call from a man with a thick Southern accent. However, it wasn't his drawl befuddling me. Instead, it was his anger regarding one of the three stadium seating sections for the upcoming ASL All-Star Game being held in Charlotte. He wanted to know why—as he put it—"in this day and age" only white people could sit in one of the sections. He explained he'd received tickets for the "White Section" despite being black.

"I thought we'd gotten past all this years ago," he said.

His words hit me like a board whacking my head, finally knocking sense into me. I thought the caller was asking about section seating by price when he was referring to Jim-Crow-segregated seating. I looked at the tickets on my desk. Sure enough, we'd printed "White Section" directly on the tickets, differentiating them from the other two sections labeled "Red" and "Blue" to coincide with the ASL's patriotic-themed colors.

After I apologized for our thoughtlessness and assured him anyone could sit anywhere, the caller graciously accepted my explanation—and presumably forgave my ignorance. Still, I pictured him shaking his head at how blind we were for using the "White Section" moniker, no matter our supreme naiveté.

Although the ticket snafu pales in comparison, the incident woke me up to how unknowing I was about the South and its history of Jim Crow laws and the associated discrimination, abuse, and killing of black people. Even then, in 1980, I was ignorant of the immense harm many African-Americans and other people of color were subjected to on a daily basis in virtually all aspects of society, including those living in Charlotte. Essentially, I was ensconced in the white section of life, only beginning to understand the extremely narrow vision this afforded me.

Three decades later, I'm still in Charlotte working in local government. One day, my boss and mentor, an African-American man, handed me an anonymous letter filled with vile, racist hatred aimed at him. By this time, I'd spent most of my adult life in the South, working decades in public service where I confronted numerous instances of racism and discrimination in the community. Yet I was stunned at the vitriol in this letter. For a minute or two, I wondered if the document was the product of someone deranged, out of touch with reality. After all, there was no denying the credentials of my boss, who'd risen to the pinnacle of his profession through talent, hard work, education, and experience.

Then my boss showed me a drawer full of such letters from people who despised him for the color of his skin and the idea of a black man in charge. With my face was turning red with outrage, I noticed my boss remained perfectly calm. This was nothing new to him. Growing up in North Carolina, racism and discrimination was part of his entire life. Instead of fueling his anger, though, the letters motivated him to succeed in spite of such hatred and the obstacles he encountered. He showed the letters to me and others so we'd better understand the depth of racial hatred and discrimination blacks and other minorities experience every day.

Once again, I was back in the white section, my vision still

The White Section

obstructed from seeing the whole playing field. Yet, this lesson from my boss also provided me a sense of clarity. Regardless how much I learn about and fight against racism and discrimination, I may never truly know it.

But I'm a Southerner now. And I am no longer innocent. •

JP McGillicuddy is a writer and photographer whose career spans the arts, professional sports, health care, and government. He is the author of seven self-published works – a novel, a memoir, and five books of his photography. He also created and wrote "The Mecklenburgers," an award-winning television program. He lives in Charlotte, North Carolina, and is a member of the Charlotte Writers' Club.

Home Cookin' Diner
by Amy Star

When we retired to Asheville, North Carolina, from the New York City area, our first apartment had such a tiny kitchen that preparing meals was not much fun. We preferred eating out. We were mostly disappointed in the downtown restaurants. They served tasty food but offered tiny portions, leaving us hungry, overspent, and feeling not warmly welcomed.

Fortunately, we discovered nearby the Home Cookin' Diner. It looked like a set from the 70's TV sitcom "Happy Days." It was everything the usual Downtown Asheville hip-dining scene was not. We found ourselves hesitating at the diner's doorway, unsure about being transported back in time and space.

"Why, come in, y'all, and welcome," a cheerful voice floated toward us. That waitress gestured for us to enter and called to my reluctant adult daughter, "Come in, Baby Girl. Don't let all the air conditioning outta here. Sit anywhere you please."

Our greeter introduced herself as Patsy, the main waitress at Home Cookin' Diner. "Don't you worry none. I'll never let your coffee, water, or soda get to a half-full moment," she promised as she constantly refilled our cups and glasses. Patsy was very reassuring and filled with down-home sensibilities. We ordered but not until after Patsy gave commentary on the menu.

"The pork chops are good today," she advised.
"Don't order the meatloaf though cause it's two days old. And the fried chicken is just plain delicious."

After taking our orders, Patsy launched into her biography as we sat wide-eyed and open-mouthed at her candor with us strangers. She started a monologue of her personal life telling us how her older daughter and her daughter's father don't get along. Patsy declared she had walked away from that fella herself and had sworn off all men, she said, "until a strong-willed man came into my life and gave me a son. Problem is that man thinks he has to have the last word, but then so do I, you know. So, I found me a gimmick. I say my last word, then I walk out of the room!" Well, we walked away, too, leaving the diner determined we would soon return for more comfort food and more gossip.

On our second visit, we were greeted like long-lost friends, and we quickly settled into what was now "our" booth. Patsy got our drinks without our even ordering. She introduced us to Rachel, another waitress at the diner. Rachel was a beautiful, young woman, and we soon learned that her three daughters showed up at the diner as soon as school let out. Rachel smiled warmly and greeted us with, "Did you know I'm going to a family reunion in Mexico?"

We tried to appear unflustered at her suddenly sharing this personal news, but we managed to say, "Oh, Mexico?" Rachel explained her grandfather was Mexican and had made frequent trips back and forth to Mexico during most of his marriage to her grandmother. "But we never knew then," she added, "that he had a completely separate, second family in Mexico. They all knew about us, but we knew nothing about them. It wasn't until Grandad died that we learned of his second, Mexican family. We'll meet them for the first time at this reunion."

We had nothing to add to that, so we purposefully turned our attention to Jasper, the cook. He doesn't want us to call him "chef." "I'm just a plain, old-fashioned cook!" Jasper said. "From Georgia originally." If Patsy was busy, Jasper was happy to deliver the food to our table himself. He hovered over us until we told him how delicious his cooking was. Then he'd give us a huge grin and go back to the kitchen.

Although most of the regular customers were Asheville-born, the diner staff still welcomed our family as one of their own. They always greeted us as friends, eager to share their good home cooking and happy to fill us in on the latest diner gossip. The food was delicious and comfortably priced. With every entree we got the Southern side-dish staples of homemade potato salad, coleslaw, and mac-n-cheese, which Jasper made in between cooking meals. The cakes were made from scratch by a local baker, and our goal soon became to sample a different cake each time we went there. Patsy gave us a 10% senior discount even though it was not an official discount day. We protested, but Patsy insisted that all seniors should get food discounts every day of the week. What was not to love?

Home Cookin' Diner

We first thought the name Home Cookin' Diner described how the food was cooked. But we soon discovered that the folks who worked there had created an atmosphere that always felt like home.

"Come in, y'all, and welcome." •

Amy Star lives in Swannanoa, North Carolina, since 2015 when she retired from the New York City area. Amy finds inspiration in the beautiful scenery of Asheville as well as the community's encouragement to create writing, art and music. Her writing group, Tale Spinners, was formed at UNCA/OLLI. At age ten, Amy's first story was published in her local newspaper. Then followed a long hiatus from publication. Amy has resumed writing and seeing her stories published since she has been living in Western North Carolina.

Bringing North Carolina Home

by Paloma Capanna

I'm still not sure how we ended up in Beaufort, North Carolina, except that we were ready to leave Upstate New York. Its taxes. Its politics. Its cabin fever winters. So, we stuck a finger on a map where the coastline showed a nearby forest.

Neither my partner Kevin nor I had traveled to the Outer Banks of North Carolina prior to what was to be an exploratory one-week trip. But, when we set foot in the two-story, brick building on Middle Lane in Beaufort, we knew we'd found our new home—and shop. I announced to Kevin: "We're going to have the most beautiful antiques shop." We put in an offer two days later, after walking barefoot on the nearby beaches amidst the wild horses.

This was February 2018. As soon as we were under contract, we set a goal to open shop on June 22, 2018, the weekend of a huge, annual old homes tour in the historic district of our town. We gave ourselves less than four months to close, complete renovations, finish inventory assembly and pricing, design and launch advertising, and open the doors.

I've been a flipper and an antiques co-op member, on-and-off, for more than 30 years. I made a to-do list and we hit estate and household sales. It was there, in a basement, that we realized how many items for sale in Upstate New York were made in North Carolina. We found everything from a fish platter marked "Seagrove, NC" to a 50s-vibe jewelry box from Kure Beach to a 1962 first edition of *Silent Spring* by Rachel Carson.

These treasures inspired us to create an important theme for our shop: "Bringing North Carolina Home." Box by box, we hauled art, art glass, pottery, used books, wooden crates, farm tools, and even a walking wheel some 750 miles and through the front doors of the shop. It seemed right. After all, so many of the items had started their journey in the hands of craftsmen from North Carolina.

I can't say it all went smoothly. One moment, in particular, had me stuck on our walkway, laughing, but ready to cry. Our four, 6-foot tall, glass display cases were delivered with a prepaid charge for delivery to the shop floor. The driver wheeled the cases to the front double-doors that I had swung wide open, only to realize I had not added palette inches to height inches when measuring. The cases would not fit through the doors. The driver dropped them quick-as-a-whip, all four, right there at the doorway, just as the wind started to kick up. Kevin and I couldn't move them, alone. In desperation, we called a man in town we barely knew to ask for help – a good-sized, former high school football player. He, in turn, called a friend of his. These kind men rushed right over. Together, with Kevin, they moved the cases through the door and into place. It was the beginning of people in town investing themselves into welcoming us and our new small business.

We describe our shop as "American Pickers" meets "Antiques Roadshow." We now travel the eastern seaboard and also westward through the Deep South to find treasured items, and then we carefully research every piece. Sharing the stories of the far-flung places we've found these North Carolina treasures makes them even more special to our local customers.

We thought adding North Carolina items to our antiques shop would educate our customers. Instead, our North Carolina customers come in and educate us on everything from the five generations of the Cole family potters in Seagrove to the ugly face jugs of New Bern native Ben Watson to the warehouses at North Carolina's own Replacements, Ltd. for bone china by Lenox, also made in North Carolina.

What we've found across the state is simply this: a deep pride in "local" craftsmanship. It may be a seven-hours' drive from our new home on the coast to reach the Smoky Mountains, but, in between, North Carolina is full of small towns and good people who keep craftsmanship alive.

We also discovered there's too much pride in these hand-crafted items to find a North Carolina seller of North Carolina goods simply giving anything away for a song. Just ask the man from Raleigh who drives more than two hours one-way to frequent our shop to buy North Carolina "business-imprinted" washboards. He'll tell you he keeps coming back because he knows how much and how far we travel, and he allows as how he can't find them anywhere else local for the right price.

Kevin and I feel blessed to now live in a state that feels as local as our new town, and to contribute to that sense of community by bringing North Carolina home. •

Paloma A. Capanna is the author of *Nearly Fifty*, a collection of essays. She most recently published short stories, poetry, and essays in *Shoal*, *Flying South*, and *Kakalak*. Paloma is a Board Member of Carteret Writers, and is a member of North Carolina Poetry Society and North Carolina Writers Network. Paloma and her partner Kevin are the proprietors of Downton Antiques, LLC (Beaufort, NC). Paloma is currently working on a group of essays titled "After the Fact," a humorous and heart-warming reflection on surviving one's parents.

.

You Got You Another One
by Paula Teem Levi

On a hot, humid, summer afternoon in 1935, my great-grandmother, Florence Woods, looked outside her kitchen window. The sky was covered in layers of dark clouds. She knew from experience those clouds foretold a thunderstorm would soon be coming. But another storm was also on its way as well, she knew. Florence had been "fetched" to a neighbor's to help deliver a third child.

Around the Poe Run community near Elkins, West Virginia, folks knew Florence fondly as "Granny Woods." They had no doctors who could make it in time to assist with a birth back in that remote "holler." Besides, Southern women were just more comfortable with a woman helping them "birth their babies." For many, Granny Woods was the authority on childbirth, highly respected. She learned how to be a midwife from her mother and from birthing her own babies.

Her granddaughter, Ruth, who would one day become my mother, traveled with her on this trip. Ruth had helped Granny Woods with birthing many times. She carried an old, worn satchel that belonged to Granny's mother. It held all the tools for birthing babies. As Ruth walked the two miles to the neighbor's house, the old satchel seemed to get heavier with each step. The wind before the storm raised dust on the road. It clung to her clothes and blew into her hair.

At the house, they found the mother already in labor. Granny Woods got busy. She took clean linens from her satchel and put them on the bed. She had the highest standards of cleanliness and hygiene. Ruth watched Granny wash her hands with homemade soap and water. Then she helped Granny put on gloves she had cleaned in alcohol.

Granny told Ruth to make a cup of hot ginger tea to give to the new mother to ease the labor pains. She pulled from the satchel some other herbs she'd grown, gathered, and dried to help with the birthing process. Ruth also pulled an axe from satchel. She placed it under the bed with the blade facing up—for "cutting the pain."

Granny Woods examined the mother to make sure the baby would enter the birth canal "head first." Assured of that and prepared for most anything, Granny Woods declared in a calm and reassuring voice, "We'll just wait for nature to take its course."

Of course, neighbors, friends, and family gathered to offer help whether it was needed or not. Granny told Ruth to take the husband and two small children outside. Granny Woods wanted the father to get water from the well just to keep him busy. Granny always said, "Keep the father out of the way."

Ruth was a good helper, but Granny did not have Ruth involved in the actual birthing. It was part of Appalachian custom that young women were not to be involved. A long labor could be a frightful spectacle, the screams and groans and the blood a good bit disconcerting.

But on this occasion, Granny Woods helped deliver a healthy baby girl after several hours. Ruth watched Granny Woods tie off the umbilical cord with a piece of twine and cut the cord with a pair of scissors, sterilized in water boiling on the wood-burning stove. She cleaned the baby with castor oil and greased the navel with an additional daub, dressing it with a dry patch of cloth baked in the oven.

That day, the new mother suddenly began hemorrhaging. Granny Woods gave the mother a cup of nettle tea to help control the bleeding. Ruth also sprang into action, having been taught in such an instance how to call on divine intervention. She began to recite over and over from the Bible, Ezekiel 16:6, "And when I passed by there, and saw thee polluted in thine own blood, I said unto thee ...Live." By grace or by incantation, the bleeding stopped, and the mother survived.

The birth of a baby was a time for celebration in the holler. So, when the news was good, the "Granny Frolic" soon began. Neighbors and kinfolk had brought in fried chicken, "cat head" biscuits, honey, molasses, home-churned butter, sweet tea, apple stack cake, and moonshine.

Granny Woods and Ruth stayed with the family for a few days to help with chores and to make sure the baby and mother were "gettin' on okay." The doctor came two days later declaring, "Well, Florence, you got you another one." He said the baby looked fine and he filled out the birth certificate. He also checked the mother and declared her ready to get back to housekeeping.

Nobody knows how many babies Florence "Granny Woods" delivered in the Poe Run Community of Elkins, West Virginia. But she was still delivering them well into the 1940s. •

Paula Teem Levi is a retired Registered Nurse living in Clover, South Carolina. She is a member of several genealogical societies. Breathing life into her ancestors' stories through her writing is her passion. She was involved in the research and writing of a published newspaper article about events in World War II. Her story, "Broken Branch," appeared in the 2019 Personal Essay Publishing Project *Exploring*.

.

A Real Small Town

by Patricia E. Watts

I was a Colorado bride in 1965, walking down the aisle to stand beside my soon-to-be South Carolina husband. Our plans were to settle in his hometown, which I had yet to see. It meant leaving my hometown of 120,000, with seven high schools, a college, and two hospitals for a "small Southern town."

Next morning after spending our first night in his hometown, he asked if I would like a tour of Mountville. The tour was only two streets that contained several houses of aunts, uncles, grandparents, two churches, an empty schoolhouse, and a country store. I asked where the sidewalks were. Was told you don't have sidewalks in the country. I'm thinking, *this can't be a real town if there are no sidewalks.* Asked how many people lived here. He said 200. I thought, that's only half the size of my high school graduating class. I admit I had a different vision of "small town."

A few days later he asked me to pick up dry cleaning in a neighboring town. The bridge across the lake was out and I had to do a long, long detour. Made it to town and found the

A Real Small Town

dry cleaners but then couldn't find my way back home. Stopped at a filling station to ask attendant for help. He grimaced and said he had never heard of Mountville. My heart sank. But he said he had a map. Looked on the map. Mountville was not on the map. I thought, *if it wasn't on the map, it couldn't be a real town.*

A few days later, my husband suggested I look for a job, saying just pick a road, any road, and it would lead to a town. I picked a road and ended up on a town square. I was going around the square when a policeman stopped me to tell me I was going the wrong way around the square. I apologized and said I had just moved from Colorado and we didn't have town squares in Colorado. He asked what I was trying to do. I said looking for a job. He asked what kind of work I did. I said legal secretary. He said an attorney on the square was looking for a secretary and if I would turn around right and go over to the police station on the square, they would help me. I thought the police station looked a lot like Mayberry, very small police station. Must not have much crime in the town. Attorney wanted to interview me so, I went over to one of the tall buildings facing the courthouse in the center of the square. As I climbed the stairs, I thought, *this is like watching an old black and white detective movie.*

Did interview. Attorney offered me the job and I accepted. Went back home, proud I had gotten a job. My husband and new mother-in-law said that I surely couldn't have gotten a job that quickly. They asked where the job was, what kind of job it was, and who it was with. When I finished answering their questions, they jumped out of their chairs and cried, "No, No, you can't have that job! You have to quit!"

I was indignant. First, they didn't think I could find a job in 20 minutes and then they said I had to quit. But evidently the attorney had two offices, and his wife had been brutally murdered in the second office. And the case was not yet closed. *It actually was like a black and white detective movie after all.*

A few days later my husband pointed me to the little country store to find some flour. I was used to shopping with a buggy and a carry out boy. I pulled up to this store, opened the heavy wooden door and swallowed hard. I thought I had stepped back in time. An old pot-bellied stove sat in the center of the store with six old men sitting around it. A single naked light bulb hung down in front of dusty shelves. One of the men got up to see if he could help me. I told him I needed some flour. When he asked me "one scoop or two," I thought, *they must not know here that it comes in little white paper bags.* Now I was truly convinced this wasn't a real town.

Now 54 years later, I have to say I wouldn't change a thing. The town now has cousins in those houses, still two churches, and more stories than you can imagine. No sidewalks, no grocery store or school yet, but I learned in time it is the people who put a place on the map. And, yes, I had moved to a real, small town after all! •

Patricia E. Watts lives in Mountville, South Carolina, where the love

A Real Small Town

of local and family history has given her a passion to write stories to pass down to her children. She has found that through stories of tragedies, tears, and triumphs and even mysteries she has a rich heritage worth telling.

Speaking of Home

by Susan Poe Hauser

I was 12 years old as I stood looking up at the old house on the hill overlooking the Yadkin River that my parents had just bought. The paint was almost gone, and many windows were broken. The house had no central heat, just seven fireplaces and some gas heaters. It sat on 11 rolling acres in Forsyth County. This would be our new North Carolina home.

Years earlier, my dad was drafted into the Army. He left his young family and fought bravely for our country in World War II and in Korea. Now he was war weary. We all had suffered. Finding this old house and land reminded him of his home where he grew up in the beautiful Blue Ridge mountains. Restoring this piece of history was healing therapy for all of us. We had a two-acre garden with lambs and peacocks and guinea fowl roaming the big yard.

Over the years, we learned so much about "River John" Conrad, who built this home for his bride, Elizabeth, in 1804. We heard many stories about the ferry he started across the

Yadkin and how he and his sons and grandsons operated it for a hundred years.

Seven generations of Conrad descendants lived in this very house, but it had fallen into disrepair. My parents rescued the old house, but I say the old house rescued them, too. And, it sent me toward my destiny too as I met and married one of those Conrad descendants.

It was August 1970 and I was engaged to be married on the front lawn in a few days. There came some heavy rains and the Yadkin River over flowed and flooded the river bottom and covered the road leading to our house. The newspaper got word of the flood and the wedding and wanted to do and interview about it. The journalist took a picture of my fiancée and me in front of the historic home. Recently when I looked at that old picture again, I saw the house as a caring presence not only over my life but the many lives that came before us. If that house could speak, I believe it would have had this to say about our wedding day:

> I am an old house, 166 years. But I am so excited! it's almost time for the wedding. I have been standing here so many years taking care of the people living within my walls. Through winter snows and spring plantings and summer rains and fall harvests, I have been here.

> Yes, I go back a long time. The Conrad family built me way before the Civil War, in 1804. They stood me tall overlooking that beautiful Yadkin River over there. I have been watching over this ol' river a long time.

I remember the ferry. I watched Mr. Conrad day after day as he ran the ferry back and forth across the Yadkin taking people and their belongings to the other side. There were no bridges then.

I do remember a sad day came when Union deserters shot Mr. Conrad's grandson at the ferry crossing. My dear Mister William! Oh, he crawled all the way up the riverbank and up the hill to my front door. He was bleeding and if I had legs and arms, I would have run to my kind master and picked him up and carried him home. But I watched over him, here in this big bedroom where he stayed three months while he was tended to, then left me.

There was that time during the Civil War when the Union soldiers took me over and used me as their headquarters. They took all the food we had stored. There were fires all over these hills where the soldiers camped. They went in my cellar and cut open barrels of molasses and brandy, letting it all flow on the ground. The ground is still sticky down there in my cellar now. A lot of my dear people left me to fight in that war.

Oh, but happy times too. Many years and many families and babies and children playing in the yard! And now there is a wedding coming up soon right here in my big, front yard. I am so happy! It has been so long since a sweet wedding. I want to be dressed up. Everyone will be looking at me, too!

Speaking of Home

Look! A lady with a camera is taking pictures of my special people, the bride-to-be and groom! Let me be in the picture! Hey, Lady! Over here! Let me be a part of this special picture, a part of this family story! It will be just the three of us. I will stand tall and watch over them. We will remember this day always.

And we did. •

Susan P. Hauser lives in Winston Salem, North Carolina. She served 50 years as a Registered Nurse. She and her husband, Michael, have four children and three grandsons. For several years, she has enjoyed participating in the writers' group, Geist Institute Women Writing Their Lives. It has helped her capture her life stories, inspirations, and remembrances to share with her family and to pass on to her descendants.

Why I Did Not Make It to the Funeral
by Scott Hooper

Funerals are big events in the South. Remembering the deceased while reuniting with friends and long-lost relatives is a cultural tradition. It is part of Southern heritage, and as such, it is an activity most certainly not to be missed. Unfortunately, I have some sort of mental block when I am told the details of an upcoming wake. I hear: "Funeral ... blah, blah, blah, two to four, blah, blah ... location." I make a mental note and file it away until I need to retrieve it.

I admit, I am also geographically challenged. When I am going somewhere for the first time, I always leave 20 minutes early for what I call "getting lost time." In 40 years of driving, I have always needed the "getting lost time" because places are never where they are supposed to be, and things never look like I picture them in my head. And, I often get left and right confused, too.

So, what I remembered from the message I recently received was "Something, something ... two to four ... something ... location." As I mentally filed this away, I thought, "two to four" is an awfully long funeral, but these are religious folks, so

Why I Did Not Make It to the Funeral

maybe they are adding something I've not thought of.

As it turns out, those little words in between the "somethings" was information I needed to know. So, thinking I have a funeral to attend at two o'clock and while I'm waiting at a stoplight at 20 minutes before 11:00, I pause to reread the message to make sure I have the address. That's when I note that the funeral is not at two o'clock, but at twelve o'clock. Uh oh. I rush home. Not having time to shower, I splash on cologne and throw on a coat and tie.

As I start my car, I quickly refer to those mental notes on how to get to the funeral home. To be on the safe side, I check the car's GPS, which I can't get to work. No problem, I go to my phone's GPS and it brings up a map. This is good. I drive and drive and finally reach a point where I think I may need to turn around, but then again, maybe I don't. So, I drive some more. I get to the road I think I'm supposed to be on and glance down at my phone which says, "Turn right," but in my mind I'm thinking, *Turn left*. Usually I have better luck with the phone than my mental notes, but this time I make the left and drive ... and drive.

Where is this funeral home that is supposed to be 15 minutes from my house? I am now 19 miles from home. That's when the light on the dash tells me "low fuel." I go back to the main road and this time make the right turn.

I find a gas station, get gas, and ask about the location of the funeral home. The guy says, "It's up the road a ways." I glance up the road and see a large building with cars lined up out front. I figure I am now too late for the funeral, but I'm in time for the procession to the graveyard. This is great because I can at least show up at the cemetery and maybe no one will notice that I missed the funeral.

I pull in behind the last car and wait a few minutes, but nothing happens. To be on the safe side, I decide to check with the car in front of me to make sure I am in line for the right procession. I get out of my car, walk up to the car in front of me and ask the lady, "What is this line for?" She replies, "I'm picking up my daughter from school." I suspect she is about to pull out her cell phone and call the sheriff's department to report that there is a strange man outside the school who does not have a child at the school. So, I ask, "Do you know where the funeral home is?"

"Yeah, it's up the road a ways."

I drive up the road, "a ways," but finally give up. I am now over an hour late. As I drive along, I glance across the road and sure enough, there is the funeral home. No one is there; the parking lot is empty. I pull off the road and set my GPS to "home" and drive the 15 minutes back to my house.

And that's why I did not make it to the funeral. •

Copyright 2020, Scott Hooper

Scott Hooper is a resident of Davidson County, North Carolina.

Why I Did Not Make It to the Funeral

He is a writer, artist, and photographer pursuing his art after his "day job." He is a member of Art for Art Sake and Associated Artists of Winston-Salem. He prefers to write poetry and has had several pieces appear in the *Winston-Salem Chronicle*. His artwork has appeared in local galleries and also in the *Winston-Salem Chronicle*.

The Enduring Feast
by Jane Rockwell

Recently, I discovered in the town where I have lived for 36 years, a house that is the mirror image of the one where my grandparents lived, 50 miles away. All the features are there, but on the opposite side. Like the house where I spent much of my childhood, this house is not what it once was. The house where Mama Bill and Pampa lived on Main Street, in Randleman, North Carolina, had a wrap-around porch with swings and rocking chairs. The porch gave me a window on the world, the small world I knew, with commentary from my family members in the rocking chairs. Our church, First Methodist, was right across the street. It took a few minutes to walk to the little downtown, and there was a sidewalk to take you there.

The house has faded, but what hasn't faded are the memories made there. And I am discovering that many of these memories reside in food. Foods, with their multi-sensory components, are efficient and extraordinary vehicles for transporting recollections and feelings. Not long ago, walking through a greenhouse at our local flower farm, I was overwhelmed by a fragrance and had to stop. I smelled Bit-o-

Honey, a candy bar I loved as a child. I was transported back to Saturday afternoons in the movie theater, slumped down in the dark red leather seats, back to Sandra Dee, "Tammy and the Bachelor," and Peter Cushing horror movies. I walked up and down the greenhouse aisle pinching off leaves and crushing them in my fingers until I found the Bit-o-Honey plant, Agastache.

On many Saturday afternoons, the mixing bowl with pink and blue trim on my grandmother's kitchen counter, usually meant butter softening for Sunday's cake—The Chocolate Cake. We all loved it; Mama Bill was famous for it. After Mama Bill was gone, family members began going through her cookbooks, recipe cards, clippings, and various slips of paper. With their eyes tearing up with every smudge in the margins, it became clear there was no recipe. No recipe for The Chocolate Cake. My mother had some idea how to make it. My aunt Peggy experimented with two different cake recipes from one of Mama Bill's cookbooks. She announced to her daughter, Karen, that she thought she had gotten it. Karen said, "Mom, you've just about got it."

My aunt Doris consulted with the daughter-in-law of Mama Bill's sister, Alese, who had made the cake, too. They must have learned it from their mother, who ran a boarding house— the house that became our grandparents' house. The Chocolate Cake was probably second nature to them. After years of research and trial-and-error, the cake was achieved. Or almost. The cake of memory that began in the cream-colored bowl with the pink and blue trim on Saturday afternoons, and appeared the next day glistening on the table—it's irreplaceable.

Mama Bill's pies were special too. There was a chocolate pie; and its cousin, a brown sugar pie. As a child, I wasn't aware that pies didn't always come out looking beautiful—that the meringue wasn't always tall, light, and airy; that sometimes it didn't quite cover the top of the pie, that the crust might fall into pieces. Now I do. A wonderful memory is having pie with the women after the Thanksgiving meal. The men moved on to football games and the younger children went to play. We cleared the dishes and returned to the dining room with pie and coffee. As they talked, I twirled the tip of my fork through the meringue and slowly worked through the rich filling. They spoke of their jobs and people I vaguely knew, not about children and their homework, their piano lessons and such. I saw my grandmother, my mother, and my aunts in a new way. I studied their mannerisms, their humor; saw that they had a kind of shorthand. It was fascinating.

Pie and coffee. I want to have more of that in my life. And it is about life, not nostalgia, life. My grandmother's cakes and pies reappear at holidays, thanks to my sister-in-law, Jodi. And thanks to my brother collecting recipes and helpful tips. My daughter-in-law, Jennifer, delights in the notes and little stars in the margins of my mother's cookbooks. I think she may be the one who solves the mystery of the persimmon pudding that so far has eluded us. At this year's Christmas gathering, the persimmon pudding lore continued to grow, to intrigue.

Family foods and their stories delight and sustain us. They, and we, endure. •

The Enduring Feast

Jane Rockwell lives in Sanford, North Carolina. She began writing seriously after a long teaching career. A one-day flash fiction workshop, with an inspirational teacher at the local community college, got her started. She continues taking classes and belongs to the Small Street Writing Group. Her poems and short fiction have appeared on the *Pittsboro-WMO* blog, on *FanStory*, and *ZenGarden.club*, where she was awarded two Grand Prizes for flash fiction. She is a member of the NC Writers' Network.

In the Hollers
by Linda Freudenberger

areening down backcountry roads meandering through Nicholas County, Kentucky, in Tony's small, 2-door sedan, I struggled to keep my breakfast down. Tony guided his car through one curve then another with ease on the narrow roads leading to his client's home. March rosebuds dotted the woods with bright fuchsia along the road in this remote part of the county. We spun the gravel heading uphill as we approached the double-wide with white and purple crocuses popping up near the porch.

Retrieving his bag of paraphernalia from the backseat, Tony led the way. This was my first home health visit as an occupational therapy student. Assigned to Tony for one week as my Level I internship, butterflies already churned in my stomach also unaccustomed to winding roads.

"For the first couple of days you will just observe and can ask me questions in the car," Tony explained. "Later I will ease you into some treatment."

"Okay but can I take notes? I asked."
"If you think you need to."

Here I was a Northern girl from Pennsylvania starting a new career in my late 30's in Appalachia. Married with two daughters ages 9 and 11, I still felt like a rookie. I WAS a rookie. One of the required OT courses was about Appalachia and its culture. This was like a foreign country to me. And, the deeper we got into the woods, the deeper the accents got. When I spoke, I felt even more like an outsider. People stared at me like I had "YANKEE" plastered on my forehead. I worried if I would ever fit in doing home health in these "hollers."

Our client greeted us at the door and led us to the darkened living room. Tony introduced me and I took a seat in an overstuffed brown recliner with a multi-colored, crocheted afghan thrown on it. The room was so dark, I could not see to take notes. I watched as Tony had the man remove his shirt; they practiced the one-handed technique to put it back on. The man's left arm dangled helplessly by his side; he walked with a limp. He'd had a stroke.

Totally engaged in the therapy session, I failed to notice a man approach me from the front door. He sat right on my lap!

Startled, I screamed, "Someone is here! It's me."

Tony and the patient burst into laughter as I shoved the elderly man off my lap and got up from the chair. He sat in the re-cliner not saying a word to me. No apology. No "Excuse me."

In the car afterward and still laughing, Tony cut his eyes toward me.

"Why on earth did that man act that way?" I asked. "I knew it was dark in there but when I screamed, he still sat on me!"

"You were in HIS chair."
"Why didn't you warn me?" I pleaded.
"Well I just wanted to see how it would all play out," Tony confessed. He explained that man was the patriarch of the household. Everyone knew that was HIS chair and no one else was allowed to sit there, not even visitors. I realized then I was being thrown headlong into the holler's habits and customs.

Other lessons came in time as well. Once Tony held a two-month-old infant lying limp in his arms. Tony asked the mother about the baby's feeding, sleeping, and general care. Then, he instructed her on positioning techniques for better feeding, having diagnosed the problem as failure to thrive. Tony asked if I wanted to hold the infant and talked to me about the muscle tone of the baby as I did.

Back in the car, he said, "You impressed me with your confidence to hold that infant. A lot of my younger students are scared to hold sick babies."

Somehow, I got through that week with the help of Dramamine® to ease my queasy stomach fighting the curvy turns of the roads. Lunch was on-the-fly with drive-through fast food so we could do all our visits for the day and get home before dark. Tony taught me about therapy techniques, Appalachian culture, and how he connected personally with his clients. I was hooked. Occupational therapy was a healing profession and the people in these remote areas welcomed us into their homes eager for the visit. This was for me.

I started as an occupational therapist in an urban hospital outpatient setting, but after 13 years of experience, I eagerly plunged back into the hollers to do home health visits in the rural counties of Kentucky. I had learned in those years a good deal about the practice, and I remembered the important things that Tony had taught me.

Number One: Don't ever sit in the old man's chair. •

Linda Freudenberger resides in Lexington, Kentucky, with her Westie, Clancy, a certified therapy dog. Linda began writing in 2017 after the loss of her husband. She took writing classes and enrolled at the Author Academy at the Carnegie Center for Literacy and Learning. Her story "The Call" was published in *Bearing Up*. Currently she is working on her memoir and a novel about a teahouse. She has also enrolled in the Poetry Gauntlet at the Carnegie Center.

.

It's the Damn Humidity
by Alice Osborn

I was born below the Mason-Dixon Line, in Washington, D.C., a North/South limbo gumbo to a French mother who hated Southern France and a father who dearly loved Charleston, South Carolina, thanks to his long ago Citadel days. My dad's Beaufort, South Carolina, ancestors fought in Petersburg in the "War of Northern Aggression" and his grandfather has an elementary school named for him on Parris Island. But, after living a quarter century in the South, I believe I can claim native Southernhood for two reasons: I have a tolerance for high humidity and I can't drive in snow. Others might also be Southern if they love their food with high ratios of sugar and salt and if their family is weird and curiously dysfunctional.

A humidity tolerance doesn't mean you enjoy the extreme weight of the air, but you deal with it, unlike my Long Island relatives who refuse to visit us in Raleigh, North Carolina, from May to September. Before I moved to Charleston in the mid-Nineties, the D.C. area's humidity didn't bother me much when I ran three miles every summer morning before I joined the Corps of Cadets at Virginia Tech as a freshman that fall.

But, no, it wasn't pretty. When I'd run up our private street, passing the first three houses, my T-shirt didn't own a dry square inch.

My French mother had immigrated to Canada and then to the D.C. area in the early Sixties after declaring she hated working for free at her older sister's souvenir shop in St.-Paul-de-Vence —an artists' haven and one of the oldest towns on the French Riviera. Fast forward a decade and some later, she's married to my dad, who's now a government bureaucrat, and they're living in D.C. Thanks to me, her mother became a grandma at age 78. In fewer than 10 extended visits over the course of 13 years, I formed a close bond with Grandma Alice, for whom I was named. I traveled to France exclusively in the summer, so I can only compare the sharp difference between the temperate clime of Grandma's house versus my wretched "slice-it-with-a-butcher-knife" hometown humidity that greeted us when my dad picked up my mom, my brother, and me from Dulles Airport at the tail end of August. Holy cow! Had the politicians sucked out all the healthy oxygen? Jet-lagged and worn out by the dramatic barometric shift, my mom wouldn't have a conversation with us for about 23 hours after we landed. I don't remember what we first ate after getting home from France, but I sure had a newfound faith in air conditioning.

As for Charleston, I'd been warned it was hot, and I clearly remembered the salt marks layered all over my black cotton dress after my dad drove us back to the D.C. area from a visit to South Carolina. (He didn't believe in air conditioning, saying it drained the car's power). I also remembered my mom throwing away half my brother's underwear because of mildew (and other biohazards) after he returned as a young teen from The Citadel's summer camp.

Yet as much as I tolerate humidity, I don't do well in snow because there must have been a magic, "fair-weather bubble" over my house because my parents never drove in the snow or rain. In my 20s, I drove a cool, red Mustang, but I had no clue my rear-wheel-drive coupe might have trouble handling a freak snowstorm in Myrtle Beach. But, I had to get to work and somehow made it by following someone else's tire tracks. After moving to Raleigh where I now live, and figuring my Mustang could competently handle snow, since it did so before, I foolishly headed out in a sudden gale and promptly slid off the road—there weren't any other tire tracks to follow!

I've lived in Raleigh now longer than in any other place on the map, and I firmly believe I'm Southern even if I don't have an accent. I've got the heritage from my dad's family and the wanderlust from my mom's side with a touch of Grandma's Continental homebody. But more than anything I can point to, I think I am truly Southern because it feels completely right to stay home at the first sign of a flurry, and I take charge of that damn humidity by carrying a dry T-shirt and underwear in my purse. •

Alice Osborn is a multi-genre author, singer-songwriter, and editor-for-hire whose most recent CD is *Searching for Paradise*. Her poetry

It's the Damn Humidity

collections include *Heroes without Capes*, *After the Steaming Stops*, and *Unfinished Projects*. Alice writes folk songs about American history that frequently return to the themes of home, identity, and yearning. She also plays fiddle, mandolin, and banjo, and is trying her hand at acting this year. She lives in Raleigh with her husband and two children. Visit Alice's website at www.aliceosborn.com.

Crepe Myrtles, Whiskey, and Cigarettes
by Amber Robinson

Crepe Myrtles line the highway and wide neighborhood streets with no sidewalks, and twanged speech drifts in the air. I moved to the South for affordable housing and a safe place to raise my family. What came with affordable housing was poor performing schools and a school system full of inequities. Everything is a fight for the marginalized. Food deserts, under-employment, transientness, book deserts, and other catch phrases are thrown around by programs and funders at meetings that are focused on solving the problems for "those people." Well, "those people" can speak up for themselves. And when they do, they tell you "we just wanted to earn a living wage, to have affordable quality childcare, schools that can nourish our little brown babies bodies and minds, and a benefits package from our employers that provides a healthy quality of life and comfortable retirement." Jobs are lost because mommy took too many days off with her sick child. Once one child gets sick, the whole household takes turns getting sick. This is a "Fire at-Will" state, so no explanation is required.

Stress and trauma perpetuated by an intolerable society and cultural oppression is big business in the South. Over 30, 000 nonprofits form every year. Programs that promise to empower, to uplift, and to educate the part of the demographic that fits their funding exponentially. This tends to be only 20% of the issue; the rest must stand aside while the program teaches the four-year-old to read but does not assist the parent in their development. Why would we want to break cycles that would put us out of work? No one enforces regulations or quality standards, so many programs just end up being something to do and not something that produces sustainable outcomes that change the trajectory of the marginalized.

Oh, the South, where oppression seems to shape shift and pick up aliases every 20 to 40 years to disguise its true intentions: slavery, Jim Crow, welfare, public housing, gentrification, redlining, gerrymandering, mass incarceration, public school, detention centers. The marginalizing and separation of people from their wealth and resources is wrong no matter what name or guise it comes under. We the people are the wealth. Build us up and allow us to thrive and this country will be great again. Greatness is when everyone has enough to eat; adequate shelter from the elements; as much knowledge as they can seek; when they are able to maintain their health; when they are given the ability to provide protection and resources for their families and when they are given freedom to pursue what makes them happy.

In the South, we have the majestic mountains to the west, the vast ocean to the east, flags fly high and Confederate monuments are plentiful. But in most cities in the still of night of summer, all you can hear are the crickets and frogs chirping out freely near waters that slaves followed to freedom and in swamps where they hid to lose their scent to dogs. Underground railroad sites are tourist attractions that are visited to bring a sense of reverence to ancestors long forgotten, but whose essences remain. We have come a long way, but have we? Church bombings and shootings and hate crimes provide a different narrative, a narrative that proves the South is still a hot bed of hate and brutality. Racist police get only a slap on the wrist for their excessive force and unequal policing activity. Why is a black defendant eight-times more likely to be convicted for the same crimes as their white counter part with the same record? We are framed, shamed, and locked away from our children to provide profitability for those who reap benefit from the penal system.

Country songs provide the soundtrack to the dysfunction—a touch of privilege and a dose of anguish stomped on by dancing boots to a country fiddle. Conditions that can only be washed down with Tennessee whiskey and obscured by cigarette smoke. Losing your wife, your house, your car and your dog are the norm for the disenfranchised.

But hope is over the horizon. Resilience runs deep in the red clay dirt that is exposed when new buildings are erected. Current victories are won not too far from historic battle sites, where reenactments are prided on being authentic. Tough-as-nails and Ford-strong is how Southerners are built. The young keep organizing, the elders keep marching, communities are still supporting, and the dreamers keep hoping. As long as the willing do, there is hope for the future, and the now is not lost. •

Amber Robinson, a Navy veteran and homeschooling mom, lives in the Triad area of North Carolina, where she enjoys connecting her community with resources and making presentations to organizations to promote equitable outcomes for the demographics they serve. She is currently supporting her 12-year-old son's efforts to write, illustrate, and publish his own graphic novel.

.

Little Rock

by Randell Jones

My cousin died this year. I didn't even know he was ill. But we'd lost touch over the years, at least the last 50. I'd known him better when I was young, he slightly older by five years. My brother and I as preteens spent two weeks several summers visiting on their family's farm outside Paris, Arkansas, getting a taste of the rural life he knew so well, he and his identical twin brother. I could never tell them apart; it was the twin who called me with the sad news.

I went to the funeral, a two-day drive from my home in North Carolina—or at least a day-and-a-half—leaving me enough time before the funeral home visitation to take in some history I thought I knew and surely should have known better. I lived through it from the next state over just across the Mississippi River, growing up in Memphis, Tennessee. But I was too young to understand it at the time. The incident happened when I was 8 in 1957. And now over 60 years later, I was standing at the spot and learning a story I never knew in a town where I was born. I was in Little Rock, looking at Central High School.

The story I knew is that the integration of Central High

School was a turning point in the desegregation of all-white schools in the South. This followed three years after the U.S. Supreme Court ruled that "separate but equal" was unconstitutional. Most people know that story as Gov. Orval Faubus calling out the Arkansas National Guard to prevent the black students from entering the school and President Dwight Eisenhower sending in soldiers to escort the "Little Rock Nine" into the school building through the line of picketing white parents and students. A famous photograph shows the students getting inside surrounded by soldiers from the 101st Airborne Division, U.S. Army, the "Screaming Eagles." And so, through the years we have turned the page in our history books and moved on. But that photograph was not the end of that story.

Generations of hardened racial prejudice had already cascaded onto the teenaged "Little Rock Nine" for a couple of weeks to that point. Thereafter, the intimidation which the adults launched outside at the beginning of the school year the students continued inside throughout the year. The Little Rock Nine were harassed in the hallways, classrooms, lunchroom, bathrooms, and locker rooms. They were shoved on the stairwells, kicked and punched from behind. The departing paratroopers were replaced by the nationalized Arkansas National Guard who reluctantly escorted the students through the halls, walking well ahead of their charges, providing no deterrence to attacks. One of the Nine was expelled for calling her tormentors "white trash" after they threw a purse filled with heavy combination locks at her head. Still, the remaining Little Rock Nine courageously persevered, excelling academically. But unable to accept federally enforced school desegregation, the school district closed Central High School for the next two school years. Students had to go elsewhere.

During my visit, I saw on that campus a broadly diverse student population, looking more like America today; but that story from 1957 is told every day by the National Park Service at the visitor center across the street for the National Historic Site. The students in the building are 60 years removed from that experience, but they have benefitted from what the Little Rock Nine endured, the true story continually told to all students there. The history lesson hits us older people differently, of course, correcting what we thought we knew.

My cousins were entering high school elsewhere in 1957, when Elvis Presley was 22, not yet drafted into the Army but already on his way to becoming "The King." The South was a different world then. Arkansas was different, too, but it changed over time; my cousins and their fellow Arkansans changed with it. I'm the one who looks back through memories fixed in time like that still photograph of the escorted students and thinks the world has stood still. Those who live in the South are changing the South. Those who will yet come to the South will change it more. The South is not a photograph, a postcard, a painting, a statue, a history book. It is alive, amorphous, organic, malleable, growing. Most assuredly the South is in motion.

Whenever we open our eyes and look around from time to time, we will surely find a different world from the one we knew before, or thought we did, perhaps when we were younger. Something happens, sometimes better, sometimes worse. Something more will yet happen still.

Gird your loins or join the parade, Southern neighbors. Change is coming. Always.

Rest in Peace, Cousin. •

Randell Jones is an award-winning history writer about the pioneer and Revolutionary War eras. Since 2007, he has served as an invited member of the Road Scholars Speakers Bureau of the North Carolina Humanities Council. He created the Personal Story Publishing Project and the companion podcast, "6-minute Stories," to encourage writers. Since 2003, he had written some 100 unpaid, history-based guest columns and letters for the editoral pages of the *Winston-Salem Journal*, many of which appear in *From Time to Time in North Carolina*. He lives in Winston-Salem, North Carolina.